The Walls

Author Picture by: Amanda Tyler

amandatylerphotography.com

1 John 3:1

"See what great love the Father has lavished on us, that we should be called children of God! And that is what we are!"

ISBN 1479124184
CreateSpace: ISBN 978-1479124183
Published and produced by Golden Lotus Inspirations
3820 Cheyenne Dr. SW
Grandville, MI 49418
Email: goldenlotusinspirations@gmail.com

Golden Lotus Inspirations

This book is dedicated to:

Sally Ann Chesebro: For being a wonderful sister, I love you.

Detective Dennis L. Mullen: For remembering Sally, so justice could be served.

Dr. Thomas Adams and Dr. Joyce DeJoung: For bringing forth the cold hard facts.

Joe Arbic: For remembering two broken little girls you met on March 9,1978.

The Calhoun County Cold Case Homicide Team: For giving me a long awaited closure and through your long hard hours and the team work, you also have given me a much needed new beginning; Carter Bright, Bill Ebberhard, Jim Gochanour, Marianne Guthrie, Bill Howe, Todd Miller, Barb Walters, Bob Wolf (Prosecutors) Michael Jaconette, Jeff Kabot, Dan Busher (Head Prosecutor) John Hallacy (Victim Advocate) Maria Markos

Judge Conrad Sindt and Judge Allen Garbrecht: For being honorable judges by up- holding the integrity of our laws that protect our constitutional rights.

A special thanks to:

Dani Pokora: For helping me to tell my story.

Amanda Tyler: For all the amazing photo work on.

Cheryl Bistayi: For showing me that I am able to bless others.

Michael K. Kivinen: For using your gifts to give me the clean slate I so needed.

(Battle Creek Enquire) Trace Christenson (Grand Rapids WXMI FOX 17) Lisa LaPlante: For proving that the media can tell the facts with integrity and with a heart.

If I can stop one heart from breaking,
I shall not live in vain,
If I can ease one life the aching,
Or cool one pain,
Or help one fainting robin
Unto his nest again,
I shall not live in vain.

~Emily Dickinson

Forward

On March 10, 1978, seven paragraphs in the Battle Creek Enquirer reported a six-year-old girl found dead in the bathtub at her home. It appeared to Battle Creek police that Sally Chesebro drowned while playing with a toy. Her mother and stepfather said it was a tragic accident. It was so much more.

A quarter of a century later, the horrific events in that house began to surface as the Calhoun County Cold Case Homicide Team was able to gather evidence that supported a story of abuse, rape and murder. That was the story Sally's sister, Nancy, told investigators.

Nancy was a year older, just seven at the time of her sister's death. She and Sally lived in a house where they were beaten and frequently placed in a tub of icy water as punishment. *"It could be for anything, even looking at them wrong,"* Nancy said. It was punishment dispensed by the mother and stepfather of the girls. That cold-water punishment was sometimes five or six times a week.

Sally's final sadistic punishment was for opening a bottle of nail polish. She was beaten, forced into a tub of icy water, and held under by her parents until she died. Stepfather David Walton and mother Bonnie Van Dam took Nancy to Sally's grave and told Nancy she was the reason Sally died.

While seven year old Nancy Chesebro could not save her sister's life, adult Nancy Spaulding did all she could to find justice for Sally's murder. Nancy confronted her nightmarish childhood, her mother, and stepfather, and told police, prosecutors, and a jury what happened inside the house at 54 Jericho Road the night her sister died.

This is the story of one woman's love for her sister, of her efforts to tell the world the truth about what happened and why Sally Ann Chesebro died. It is a story of how one sister kept her promise and fought for justice.

~Trace Christenson~

Intro

A cold case is a description given to a homicide that has gone unsolved for so many months/years because all clues have gone cold, hence the term, "Cold Case."

We have movies that are based on true stories, in which names have been changed to protect the innocent. We also have the documentary shows like A&E Cold Case Documentary that comes into your life to help you to tell your story on film. Then in turn uses these documentaries to help train other individuals of law enforcement.

Due to the fact that there's none or very little funds for cold case teams, old homicides fall to the wayside, so those cases are put on the back burner and if something comes up is brought back out. Because of this, families are left with a hole that will not be filled.

Some people also say, "It's the past, just let it be." Because we are people, we vote and our votes are voices to tell those who write the laws what we want money to be spent on.

I would understand this thinking if I was a person that had not been touched by a homicide, but sadly, I have been so what I see is different. Just because something is the past does not mean it is gone. There is a long list of emotional and physical issues that stem from not having the justice of a solved homicide.

Speaking from my experience only, I know that cold case teams are very important not just to the individual, but for the community as well.

Before the Calhoun County Cold Case Team of Battle Creek, Michigan came into my life, I was having a hard time functioning at home and in society.

I remember my friend Cheryl asking me a few months before the cold case team came to me, "Nancy, percentage wise, because of your childhood, how much of your energies are spent just keeping your head above water?"

Without blinking an eye I said, "ninety-five percent."

Cheryl says, "Do you realize that only leaves five percent of yourself to give to your family?" Goodness, did that ever make me think, it sure did put things into perspective.

A few months later the cold case team was at my front door, throwing me the life preserver I so badly needed.

Taxpayer's money well spent, for now my kids have a healthier mother and I am now a more productive member of society. Not only that, a solved, "Cold Case" tells the community that if you murder someone you will eventually be caught.

Cold case teams do not give just any kind of closure, for it is a closure that helps one to move on in life … a new beginning.

Chapter One

"Let the memory live again."
~Memory-from the Broadway musical, Cats~

You know that saying, "You don't know what you really had until it's gone." Oh my, how true that really is. For it seems that the common lesson I am to learn on my life path is just that, for every time I lose a treasure that I have taken for granted, I get a bit closer to perfect knowledge of knowing that in order to really appreciate the next treasure I need to take those feelings of loss with me.

As I sit in front of my computer doing the usual web surfing. I decided to look up the Calhoun County Homicide Cold Case Team to see what was up with the team.

My heart sank as I read that the team is going to be dismantling on January 1, 2010 only after eight short years. How sad, for Cold Case Teams are very important for those who have suffered the pain of losing a loved one due to homicide and not just any homicide , but ones that are unsolved.

As I sit and remember; I cry for I feel yet another loss, a loss for those who were not given the peace of mind, the justice that I have received, that they so deserve.

As I get out the items that I have saved during my time of justice, I am remembering the day my stepfather and mother were arrested.

I was sitting in the health center waiting for my number to be called for blood draw. My phone rings. I look at the caller ID and as I read Cold Case, I think about letting it go to voice mail. Instead I decide to listen to my inner self and I answer the call.

"Nancy … David, and Bonnie are being arrested right now and will be arraigned in a few hours," says Barb Walters.

"Get to Battle Creek as soon as possible for the arraignment."

I go to the medical assistant and give her my number that held my place in line.

"Sorry I have to go."

As I hurry to my car, I call my friend who is a Fox news reporter, Lisa LaPlante.

"Bonnie and David are being arrested right now and will be arraigned in a few hours," I tell her as I am unlocking my door.

"Yes, I know Nancy. I am on the road right now, how are you doing?"

"I'm okay, just numb. Really overwhelmed right now."

"Everything will be okay Nancy, drive safe and I will see you when you get to Battle Creek."

One minute I was in Grand Rapids, the next in Battle Creek, an hour and an half car drive away and no memory of how I got there.

When I got to the courthouse Maria Markos, my victim advocate, met me at the back door so media and public would not see me.

"Sorry," says Maria, "But we have no time to sit down to brief you. Briefing has to be done as we walk to the courtroom for Bonnie and David are being brought into the courthouse right now."

Maria and I got out of the elevator to flashes of lights from the zoo of media individuals that were there waiting to record every breath that came from me. As Maria guides me through the media, I smile at Lisa as I go into the courtroom.

As I sat there on the bench in the courtroom, the media was bustling in and out as if there was someone important around. As microphones were being put into my face, questions-tossed out to me in hopes that I would comment, Maria would be my peace of mind by telling the media "no comment" and kept the media at a respectful distance.

"All rise…"

As I stood, I looked at the television screen to see that Bonnie was being brought in to be arraigned by satellite.

"You are being charged in the March 9, 1978 murder of Sally Ann Chesebro, how do you plea?" commands the judge.

"Not guilty."

Then it was David's turn.

"How do you plea?"

David looks around as if the judge's voice was the voice of God.

"Not guilty."

Maria and I left the courtroom to go to her office.

"Can you make it in tomorrow to talk to the prosecutors?"

"Yes…just tell me what time."

"See you at ten?"

"Ten it is."

Since I told Lisa LaPlante that I would do an interview after I was done at the courthouse, I called her from my mobile to meet me so that she could follow me to Sally's grave to do the interview.

Lisa asked basic questions, I answered honestly.

The interview was done when we looked over across the graveyard and saw Melissa Dumas coming towards us. Melissa had asked for an interview in which I said no that I will another time. Lisa knew of this and that I did not want to give an interview to anyone else that day.

"Nancy, you do not have to say anything that you do not want to."

"I know."

As Lisa hugs me she says, "goodbye and if you need anything of me, please call."

"Thank you so much Lisa."

"Just a few questions please" says Melissa.

"No!"

"This will only take a few minutes."

"I said no and not only that I already told you earlier that I did not want to do an interview with you right now but will later; but here you are trying force one and I really do not appreciate the fact that you are disrespecting my wishes…bye!"

As I get into my car, slam my door to put emphasis on how upset I was that she had followed me as if I was a movie star who was caught drinking and driving.

The next day Cheryl drove me to Battle Creek to meet with Jeff Kabot, the prosecutor for Bonnie, and Michael Jaconette, prosecutor for David.

I stopped at a gas station to use the bathroom and to buy a bottle of water.

As I stood there waiting to pay for my water, I looked around and there it was; my picture on the front page of the Wednesday May 22, 2002 local paper with the headline: "Couple arraigned in 1978 death of child" by Trace Christenson in *The Battle Creek Enquirer.*

I got to the prosecutor's office. As I sat in Maria's office with Cheryl at my side, I rock back and forth to bring comfort to myself.

Jeff and Michael came into the office to tell me what to expect and how things usually go. After this, Jeff left the office while Michael stayed.

I looked at Michael as tears came to my eyes and said, "Michael I do not know what people are going to expect to see from me, but I do know that when he or anyone ask questions of me they will be talking to a seven year old and not an adult."

"All anyone wants is for you to be yourself and do the best that you can, you came a long way, and frankly we are all amazed at how far you have come. You have already exceeded our expectations for we expected someone not all together because of what you went through; and what we got is someone who has risen to the top," says Michael as he pats me on the back and smiles an approving smile at me.

After the meeting with Michael, I was so tired that I slept all the way back to Grand Rapids.

As I packed up my memories, I decided to fix a cucumber sandwich and pour a cup of coffee for a quick lunch before getting my kids from school.

On the way to the school, I remembered the last time I was at the Calhoun County Prosecutor's office. I was giving the interview of a lifetime, an interview that once again put me in the public's eye.

I remember that the night before the interview was as any other I have experienced at work. As a hotel night auditor I got the usual request for towels, deodorant and even tampons, which one may have forgotten to pack.

As the reports are printing, I locked up the pool house, picked up room service trays and assigned wake up calls, but really all I had on my mind was what was going to happen in the morning.

As I plugged away at the numbers to make sure the day's receipts were balanced, I also went through my mind systematically on what I have to do before my one and a half hour drive from Grand Rapids to Battle Creek.

I am thinking about how I have to get off work at eight in the morning and need to be in Battle Creek by eleven, but before that I have to be at Cheryl's at nine to get into her car. I know I have to go to the YMCA, which is next to work, to take a shower and get ready because I did not have enough time to go home.

My morning relief, Maya, came in her usual self with her eyes red and watery due to her seasonal allergies and not feeling a hundred percent, but I was just grateful she was there early.

I felt like a child waiting in front of the fireplace on Christmas Eve with wide eyes hoping to sneak a peek of Santa.

I got out of the shower and dried off, put on a new outfit that I bought just before going to work. It was the first time I saw myself in the outfit. I was not sure if I liked it. I was used to wearing all black most of the time and this outfit was white pants and a white top with a purple sweater.

When I looked into the mirror, I was not sure who that person was. When I looked into the eyes of the person I saw in the mirror, I said, "that's Nancy" but, like many other women in a new outfit, I needed a second opinion. I quickly drove back across the parking lot to work so I could ask Maya for an honest opinion.

"Do I look okay?"

"Yes, you look nice and springy. Now go before you're late."

On the way to Cheryl's I went to Dunkin' Donuts, got coffee and bagels, which were our best friends that we would start our days with.

While on my way to Cheryl's, my feet started feeling like they were on fire. The night before, my daughter had a friend over. I had to take her home and when we got out of the car, it seemed like a million mosquitoes had decided to move into my car. It literally took me driving my car a few miles away from the wetlands, pulling over on the side of the road and opening the doors and windows to shoo them out. In the meantime, the invaders were stinging away at my feet and even in between my toes.

With my itchy feet, warm bagels, and hot coffee I pulled up in front of Cheryl's house. I went into the house and Cheryl's at the top of the stairs.

"Make yourself at home."

Cheryl came down the stairs and into the kitchen, got her bagel and coffee and looked at me.

"Well, are you ready?"

I was unable to say anything; I just looked over at her and cried. She embraced and comforted me.

"Now, Nancy I'm here for you and know that if things get hard, you can always ask for a break."

When the two of us get talking, we just talk and at times I can't remember the conversation, maybe because it is not what is spoken that counts. It is what the heart has to say that counts. I believe that the heart speaks much louder than the mouth ever can, because the heart speaks the truth.

At this time, Cheryl and I have known each other for five years. What once was a professional counseling relationship has turned into the ultimate friendship.

I needed her to do what she is good at, to be by my side and make me laugh. She joked that she was going to bounce around behind me when I was on camera, much like a sports fan caught in the background of an interview with a famous athlete. But this was no sporting event.

That day, a part of my life would be relived, the television series, A&E "Cold Case Files", wanted to film my story, a story that began over a quarter of a century ago.

Most people would not choose to have their fifteen minutes of fame this way, but just like a lot of other people, I did not have a choice.

The producer took me back in time to the day my sister Sally was murdered.

Cheryl, the crew, and I eventually ended up in front of 54 Jericho Road.

When I was a child, it was a middle class neighborhood with teachers, and bankers and Sunday school teachers and where other so-called respectful individuals lived.

However, behind closed doors, the stories were different, especially in our home. After over twenty-five years, I now know that this was not my fault.

From the day Sally died alone in an icy cold bath, my parents blamed me. Sally took a punishment for something I did; they said it was my fault that she got the cold bath treatment and not me. They said it was my fault she died in that tub.

Now the evidence has proven otherwise. After all, I was only seven years old and she was my best friend. How could our parents, who were Sunday school teachers, put their two little girls through such sexual, physical, and emotional trauma? Why did it take twenty-five years to find out the truth?

Standing outside 54 Jericho Road as an adult, I can now see reality. The once well-groomed yards and freshly painted houses that lined the streets are now dilapidated and riddled with crime. The outsides of these houses have now caught up with the horrors of the insides.

Chapter Two

"Oh I realized Nancy it's your birthday, the whole universe joins me, wishing you happy birthday."
~Dr. Parasuram Ramamoorthi~ (a poem written for me)

I was born April 26, 1970 at Lakeview General Hospital to Bonnie Lee (Doty) Chesebro and Benjamin Charles Chesebro. My mother was nineteen and my father was thirty-five. I was supposed to be a boy and then two girls were to be born after my birth. This was my mother's idea of "the perfect family."

Well, I was not a boy and my mother resented that fact and refused to name me so my grandmother, Bonnie's mother, Lottie (Boyer) Howard came to the hospital and named me Nancy Marie Chesebro.

When I was growing up, my mother would always hold it against me that I wasn't a boy and let it be known from day one that she hated the fact that her oldest was a girl.

On December 27, 1971, my sister was born in Community Hospital. My mother again, was hoping for that boy, again refused to name her baby girl; Lottie came to the hospital and named her Sally Ann Chesebro.

When I was four months old, my aunt Lisa came to visit Ben, Bonnie and me. She found me lying in the crib with maggots crawling all over me in my ears, nose, and mouth.

When Aunt Lisa picked me up to clean me she found that not only was I soaked, but I also had old BM in my cloth diaper.

Aunt Lisa took me to the bathroom to clean me, she got sick and mad to see that when she took my diaper off that the tender skin on my bottom was so raw that it was peeling, bleeding and oozing from sores.

She took me to a doctor for this was beyond what she could do for me. The doctor took care of the sores and gave my aunt medicine and cream to help the healing.

My grandmother Edith Thurston, Ben's mother would always tell me that no matter what I was always a happy child; I sometimes wonder if by knowing that I was a happy child if that was her way out of not turning her son and daughter-in-law into authorities.

Just because a child is happy does not mean that the child is being treated right, but what it does mean is that the child has a strong spirit.

It is July 1974 and I am four years old and singing, "Shall We Gather At the River." I am standing at the banks of a river and I am so happy I could just explode because I love Jesus and I know Jesus loves me too.

As I walk into the river the chilled waters going up to my waist, I thought to myself, "I'm supposed to be afraid of cold water, but something is making me feel safer then I have ever known." I keep walking until I am where I am supposed to be.

"Do you love Jesus with all your heart and are you ready to be born again?"

I look deep into the pastor's eyes as if I was looking for a treasure and reply, "Yes!"

The chilled waters were now covering me and then it was done, like a flash of lightning. The pastor smiles a warming smile and says, "Good job."

I then join Sally, my grandparents, David and Bonnie and the rest of the church in singing, "Are You Washed in the Blood of the Lamb."

A few weeks pass and my uncle John, my mother's brother, is visiting us.

John is wrestling around with me and tickling me so hard that I am trying my best not to bite, but by instinct, I bite him.

Uncle John is so mad at me that he stands up and punches me in the chin, splitting it wide open. I must have blacked out for the next thing I know I am in the emergency room being held down to receive stitches without a clue of how I got there.

We did not like Uncle John; he was mean to us like our mother and David.

When I got the stitches out of my chin, Sally and I had chickenpox. I am sick, sicker then Sally. When I am sick, I like to lie on the floor and sometimes under my bed. I am lying under my bed sleeping when Uncle John comes up to the room with our lunches.

"Where is Nancy?"

"She's under her bed."

I do not know why, but Uncle John kicks me right in my right side. I throw up right away. He then sets my tray on the bed as he reaches under the bed and pulls me out by my hair.

I crawl into my bed, crying into my food making it salty and soggy, and eat my grilled cheese and chicken noodle soup.

When I was five, Sally and I had to get stitches in our fingers. David and Bonnie were going to the hospital to visit our great-grandmother. As we were on our way, my sister and I were picking on each other and our parents were yelling at us to stop, but we just kept picking on each other.

When we got to the hospital my mother says, "Put your fingers right here," pointing to the inside of the car door.

She purposely slammed the door on our fingers for our punishment; she then took us into the hospital for stitches and then to our great-grandmothers room to visit her.

Later, when I was six, Bonnie asked me to take the trash out.

As I lift the bag, a lid from a can slices the inside of my knee.

"Mom, my knee is cut and bleeding a lot."

"You are okay, just take the trash out."

I do as I am told; upon my return to the house, my whole leg is covered in blood.

"Get cleaned up because Grandma Honey will be here soon."

When Grandma Honey arrives, the wrapping is soaked in my blood, with no white spots to be seen.

She insists that I be taken to the emergency room.

Getting these stitches was not fun. I was fighting so hard that two nurses and Bonnie were holding me down while the doctor gave me a shot to knock me out just so that they can work on me.

A month later, the stitches are gone and my sister and I are going to my father's for a visit.

On the way back home, Ben, my father, takes us to Mr. Don's, a local fast food restaurant, for lunch. After washing a cheeseburger and fries down with a root beer, my father walks Sally and I back home to 54 Jericho.

On the way, we have to pass the city metal scrap yard. Just before this yard there is an overpass.

"Follow me girls."

We are huffing and puffing up the cement wall to reach the top. It is flat, and my heart is beating fast. "What's going on...?" I am thinking to myself, "Why are we going up here? This isn't the way home." I am having the overwhelming feeling that this is not going to be good at all.

We are at the top and father tells me to lie down. I do as I am told.

Next thing I know, my father is taking his hands up my dress, pulling my white tights and underwear down around my ankles.

I am so scared. I cannot look at him. Instead, I look to my left at the cement wall where Sally is sitting watching this whole thing.

As I am looking at Sally, my father bends my knees up, and my feet are now somewhat flat on the ground, my legs open wide.

I am laying there with my bare bottom on the warm cement as my father lays himself on top of me. I am feeling his privates go inside mine; the pain causes tears to run down my cheeks. I am also having pain on my soft little bare bottom rubbing against the cement as my father moves inside and outside of my privates his weight laying upon my body. The whole time I do not say a thing, I look over at Sally with tears running down my face.

When father is done with me, I reach down my shaking legs to my ankles to pull up my underwear and tights. As I reach, I can feel blood on my back and bottom where I have cuts and bruises from the ground. I see my father's shoes and I hear the zipping of his pants.

I run down the street as fast as I can until I am outside the fence of the scrap yard. I slide down with my hurting back against the fence to a sitting position, my knees to my chest and my arms holding tight to my knees, burying my head into my knees and crying.

My father and Sally catch up with me.

"Let's go."

I get up and start to follow as he leads Sally and I back to Jericho Road.

A few weeks had passed, when father came back to Jericho Road to pick Sally and I up for another visit.

Sally and I are not ready to go, we are going up to our bedroom to get ready. I look at Sally with tears in my eyes, remembering what happened last time we visited father.

"Don't let him touch you and I won't let him touch me, just say no."

"Okay."

We are coming down the stairs and we are scared.

Father smiles at us and says, "Are you ready to go?"

We nodded our heads yes and go out the door with him.

We are at his apartment, a one-room place that is very small. His apartment is on the third floor and there is only one bathroom on the floor at the end of the hall that is shared with all the other apartments on the floor.

Sally and I are sitting at the table, close to the bed. We are eating our lunch, which is cold cereal. Father sits on the bed and looks at us in a way that makes us scared.

"Come here Nancy."

"No."

"I said come here."

"No!"

He looks at Sally and says, "Come here."

Sally, who did not want to disobey, slowly goes over and sits on the bed next to him.

Father reaches over and lays Sally on her back.

Sally lays back and looks over at me and I can see fear in her eyes. I start to feel sick.

My father's hands are going up her dress and all that is going through my mind was what my father did to me last time we visited him. Sally sat and watched father hurt me and I did not want to watch her get hurt.

I run out the door, into the hall and I notice to my left an open window.

I go up to the window and notice there is no screen.

I decide that I do not want to deal with this; I go out the window onto the ledge, getting ready to jump.

"Come in right now Nancy," says my father.

"I am not going to, unless you leave Sally alone now."

Sally then comes to the window, crying and begging me to come in.

I look at Sally and decide to come back in, thinking, "I can't leave Sally to deal with the people that hurt us all alone."

I am back in the hall and I look at my father and tell him, "I want to go home right now." He tries to talk me out of it, but I tell him, "I want to go home now!"

When we got home, Grandma Honey was there.

Grandma Honey is David Walton's mother; David is our stepfather. We call her Grandma Honey because that is what everyone called her.

We were told the story of when David was a little boy, how every time he would try to say "mommy" it would sound like "honey" and that is how she got labeled with the name Honey.

My father tells everyone that Sally and I wanted to come home early and leaves.

Grandma Honey looks at us, "why did you want to come home early?"

I tell her what had happened in father's apartment; she says not to worry and that it will be taken care of.

It is the next day and these people are coming to talk to us about what happened. They talk to me and Sally and when they get done answering questions they tell us that we do not have to visit our father anymore.

It is now winter, our mother bakes a cake and gives us a slice.

The next day, we get home from school and Sally and I are hungry. Mother and David are in bed sleeping, we know that we are going to be in trouble if we wake them up to ask if we can share the last piece of cake.

Therefore, we share the slice of cake without asking. When Mother wakes up, she sees that we ate the last of the cake.

She comes over to Sally and I, looks down at us, takes her fist and punches both of us in the stomach.

As we are trying to breathe again, our mother is tearing my shirt off.

"Get undressed."

Sally and I look at each other and we do as we are told while thinking, "Will it be the snow or the cold bath punishment?"

We hear the front door open; we start to cry very hard because if there were any time we would choose the cold bath punishment, it would be now.

We cry all the way to the front door and then we walk outside.

"You know what to do."

We sit in the cold snow with no clothes on; Mother has her winter coat on and is standing on the porch yelling at us.

"You're pigs and pigs live outside."

Mother tells us to crawl and roll around in the snow and act like pigs.

She finally lets us back in the house and tells us that we ate enough already and that we are to go straight to bed.

It is now the summer, Mother and David lock Sally and I in our bedrooms on weekends and in summer. Sally and I get up before our parents and they do not want us to roam around the house while they sleep all day.

When we are locked in our rooms, we talk to each other through our bedroom doors, not realizing that our parents could hear us through the floor. They came running up the stairs, David is in Sally's room, and our mother is in my room.

We are getting beat, so bad that there is blood coming from our mouths and noses.

Mother tells us to come out to the hall. Sally and I are standing with our backs to the stairs.

Mother says, "We never want to hear you talking again when you are locked in your rooms." She then pushes both of us down the stairs.

We go back to our rooms. I lay down in my bed, bleeding all over my pillow and crying and gagging on my blood. I can hear Sally, crying just as hard as I am. I feel sadder for her than for me.

We had learned our lesson and we stayed quiet as can be.

Sally and I are hiding junk food, mostly old and half-eaten, that we get from what mother and David do not eat from the kitchen.

We would hide the food in our closets so we could eat when we got locked into our rooms.

When it is Sunday, we get a break from our rooms; they would make sure we were up in time for church. We sat in our parents' Sunday school classes, listening to them teaching us God's word, how we need to be good and treat people the way we want to be treated.

When we get back home from church, we are locked back in our bedrooms.

A real big problem we have when locked in our rooms is going to the bathroom. We open our windows and sit on the window ledge and pee out the window. If we have to go number two, we hold it until we cannot anymore and we go in our pants. Sometimes we hold it so long that we get sick to our stomachs. The pain gets so bad that we throw up all over the floor.

As we make sure to clean up the mess, we are using dirty clothes in hopes that our parents, if they find out, will not get too angry. Sometimes we are able to sneak the clothing into the basement and toss it on top of the ever-growing mountain of dirty clothes.

I remember, starting at the age of four, David would have Sally and I put his privates in our mouths.

As our mother sits and watches, us suck on David, Sally and I throw up because some white stuff was being put into our mouths. We got a beating because we threw up and because we made a mess all over David and the bed.

We had to clean the bed and give David a bath while our mother was there making sure we did it right.

Sally and I were finally got used to David and our mother doing this to us, we knew what to expect every time.

"Rubber ducky" was a nickname given to Sally from our mother because Sally sometimes wet her pants.

Sally and I went into the store with our mother while David waited in the car. We are standing in line and Sally pees her pants right there.

When we got into the car, mother tells David what happened in the store. They start to tease Sally, calling her "rubber ducky." Sally starts to cry and I made her cry worse because I start to drawn pictures of little ducks on the window of the car.

Mother saw what I had done.

"Good drawing Nancy" and pointed it out to David.

When I got home, I feel bad.

"I am sorry Sally."

"Okay."

I give her a hug as I promise her that I will never do it again.

Chapter Three

"Everyone can see we're together...And we fly just like birds of a feather."
~ We Are Family- by The Pointer Sisters~

I learned some hard lessons in my life before I turned seven, but I never knew that at the age of seven my heart would be ripped out of my chest. The feelings I had on March 9, 1978 no seven year old should have experienced. Of course, there is a lot that young children should not have to experience especially in the hands of their parents.

I often asked myself as I was growing up, "why can't my parents love me?" Now as an adult and a mother myself I look back with the hope that my parents did love me, they just did not know how to show love to my sister and me.

In addition, to think all I ever wanted was, "I am sorry Nancy and I love you," I never heard I love you from any of my parents. How sad to bring into the world two beautiful souls and never tell them you love them.

I am on the floor playing cards with Sally, the television is on, and mother is calling to me from the chair behind me in the living room. I cannot hear her right away, so she throws an Amway Seespray can at me and it hits me in the head.

"I told you to go and put my clothes in the dryer."

I go to the basement with my right hand holding my head because it feels like it is falling off. I bring my hand away from my head and running down the side of my face was blood.

"Mom, my head is bleeding!"

"I don't give a damn, just do what I told you to do."

I am dizzy and walking back to the living room, so that my mother and David can see the blood.

David goes to bring the car out to the front of the house and mother is calling her brother John to ask him to meet us at the hospital.

David honks and we get into the car to go to the hospital.

I must have passed out because the next thing I know I am waking up in the bed of the E.R. My mother is standing on one side of the bed and the doctor and nurses are standing on the other side.

"She fell down the basement stairs."

"She is going to need stitches," says the doctor.

I am so scared because I have had many stitches, but this time it is in my head. I am fighting and out of control.

The doctor is concerned, "She needs to calm down."

The nurse gets a needle ready and looks at me.

"Don't worry honey, everything will be okay," then gives me the shot.

I wake up in the arms of my uncle John; he is carrying me into the house and lays me on my bed.

Thursday March 9, 1978; it starts off like any other day with mother standing at the end of the stairs.

"Get up, it is time to get to school!"

Today is going to be a half day of school because today is parent-teacher conferences, but we still meet our friend Rachael and her twin brother John to walk to school with. My friends like half days, but Sally and I don't because we feel so much safer at school and most of the teachers are kind to us.

School is out and we are walking with our friends again. Rachael and John are happy, but Sally and I are not. I am thinking about how we did not get lunch because of it being a half day and most of the time the only time we get to eat is breakfast and lunch at school.

Sally and I get home and have to leave right away for conferences.

We are hanging out in the halls of the school, mother and David are sitting at the table with the teacher, and they look so normal.

We get back home and our mother and David go straight to bed without cooking any dinner.

Sally and I are sitting in the living room playing and watching television; we are getting very bored.

"Hey Sally, I am going to ask mother if we can paint our fingernails."

I am tiptoeing to the bedroom door; I can feel my heart beating because I know that I could get into trouble waking them.

"Mom...mom."

"What?"

"Can we use some nail polish?"

"Wait until I get up and I will put it on you."

"Okay."

Walking back to the living room, I feel relieved because I did not get into trouble for waking our mother. I am thinking that today they are in a good mood.

We are getting tired waiting for mother to wake up; I go into the bathroom under the sink and pull out her Avon bag because mother sells Avon.

I open the case of nail polishes. I look at all the colors which we are not allowed to wear because we Baptist. I take out the clear, bring it to the living room and I put it on Sally and I.

I open the nail polish.

"Put your hand on my leg."

I can paint her nails and then I paint mine, then I put the nail polish back.

We go back to playing and watching television; we hear the bedroom door open.

"Who got into my nail polish?"

Sally and I look at each other and shrug and at the same time say, "I don't know."

"David, come here!"

Bonnie tells David what is going on; they then sit in their chairs, which also had ottomans in front of the chairs, Sally is standing in front of David and his ottoman and I am in front of our mother.

Bonnie and David keep asking back and forth, "who got into the polish?"

Sally and I keep saying, "I don't know."

We are crying so hard.

"I did it!" cries Sally.

I am trying to tell our parents that I did it, but they are not paying any attention to me.

Mother grabs my baton and whacks Sally across the legs; she falls to the floor.

Sally tries to get back up David pushes his ottoman into her; she falls back to the floor.

Now our parents are over Sally, beating her; I am crying.

"Stop it…I got into the nail polish…leave her alone!"

They did not hear me; they just keep beating her.

Mother looks at me, "go fill the bathtub with cold water."

"No…I won't!"

She slaps me.

David yells at me, "Do what you are told…now!"

I go and run the cold water. As the water is running, I go back into the living room.

Mother is yelling at Sally.

"Why did you get into the nail polish?"

Sally just cries.

Mother hits and pushes her all the way to the bathroom.

Mother pushes her onto the floor at my feet, Sally looks up at me, we make eye contact, and my heart is breaking.

All I am able to do is cry and say, "Sorry" then bow my head in shame.

I go to sit on the sofa, mother, and David goes back to bed.

The television is still on and "I Love Lucy" is showing. Lucy would always make Sally and I laugh, but not today.

I am sitting on the sofa crying, mother, and David after sleeping for a bit goes into the bathroom. Some time has passed and I hear them go back to their bedroom.

I am going to go to the bathroom; I am going to do something in the bathroom so Sally can get out for a little bit and warm up. We are not allowed in the bathroom together because of noise since our parent's bedroom wall shares with the bathroom.

Knowing this, Sally and I made a pact when our parents started to use cold bath punishments; when there is one in the tub, the other pretends to use the bathroom.

"Sally...Sally...Sally, come out so I can use the bathroom."

Thinking that she could not hear me, I walk into the bathroom to tell her to get out.

I walk into the bathroom and see Sally lying face down in the tub, confused and scared I call out her name.

"Sally...Sally what's wrong?"

I move closer to the tub, I see that she is not moving; I quickly go to the tub and reach into the icy water to pull Sally's head out of the tub, I grab her under her arms.

"Sally say something, please say something!"

There is nothing but gurgling sounds; I think she is trying to say something to me, but I cannot figure out what it is.

I yell and cry.

"Mom...dad...mom...dad ... Please come! Something is wrong with Sally!"

Mother comes into the bathroom, she carries Sally to the kitchen; David then comes and carries her to the dining room.

David is doing CPR; mother is walking back and forth.

"What should we do?" Mother asks David.

I answer back, "call for help!"

Mother decides to call her mother.

"Hello mom - something bad has happened, Sally had an accident in the tub, she won't move or speak ... okay, mom"

My mother hangs up the phone and calls the ambulance.

While waiting for help to arrive, mother and David dry and dress Sally.

David reached to grab a towel in a nearby pile; our house is always a mess.

The ambulance people are here, they walk right past me. Mother and David moves into a corner to watch.

Mother rides in the back of the ambulance; David drives behind them. I am sitting in the front seat crying and scared and David is talking to me.

"Listen."

"If anyone asks you what you know, it is that Sally was taking a bath and nothing else."

I glare at David.

"I mean it Nancy; don't say anything else or you will be hurt like Sally was."

"Okay."

We pull into the parking lot of Lakeview General Hospital.

The ambulance is already there. I walk through the door, I look to my left, and laying there on a stretcher in the waiting room was Sally. I get very upset and I start to cry.

My grandparents, my mother's mother and stepfather, Hank and Lottie were there.

I am starting to yell, cry, and run to Sally. My grandfather is holding me back.

"Let go of me now…I want Sally!"

Grandmother looks at grandfather.

"Get her out of here."

"No, I want to stay with Sally!"

My grandfather takes me to another hall where there are three chairs.

We are sitting, waiting for someone to come and get us. I can hear my cries eco in the halls while I wait.

After waiting for a while, pastor Gowen comes to get us.

Gowen looks down at me and says, "Come with me, I will take you to where everyone else is."

Pastor Gowen leads us to this small room.

I walk into the room and my mother and David reach out to hold me.

I did not want them to hold me so I go right over to Mrs. Gowen and sat on her lap and cry.

The door opens and a doctor comes in, we all are looking at him.

"I am so sorry, we tried everything we could. We just won't able to save Sally...I am sorry."

When he leaves, I cry so hard and loud that I feel like I am going to be sick, so I just bury my head into Mrs. Gowen.

It is the day before Sally's funeral, my mother and her mother are talking about what Sally was going to be buried in, and they cannot agree.

My mother brings a dress down and it has stains, holes and smells awful.

"Aren't you ashamed that you don't make sure the girls have clean clothes? I never took care of you like this."

My grandmother is right for I have seen pictures of my mother as a baby and a little girl; she was so cute and always so clean.

"Forget it...I'll go out and buy something!"

My grandmother takes me to K-Mart to help pick out a dress. It is a pretty shade of pink and the bodice is covered in beautiful lace. We then went to the Royal funeral home to drop off the dress.

What a perfect place for Sally to have her funeral with a name like Royal because when I saw her in her dress that is what she looked like...royalty.

She looks like a sweet princess laying there in her deep sleep waiting for her prince to come to give her a first kiss of true love to break the spell she was in and she would live happily ever after.

There is the child part of me that wants to believe that her prince is going to come on his white horse, but I know that fairytales really do not come true.

Many of my schoolmates were allowed to be children and free.

I am thinking of Amy, who has beautiful, clean, short, straight, blond hair that shines when the sun shines on it. I am finding comfort in thinking about classmates because they do not have to be at a funeral.

I now know Sally is in heaven sitting on a cloud looking down at me. I hope she is trying to figure out a way to get back to me so the aching in my heart would go away.

I need my sister in my life; if there was one thing I know right now, it is that.

I am at the funeral in dirty clothes; I was not even wearing a dress.

My mother has me wearing pants covered in dirt and holes and a t-shirt

My grandmother is very upset and shakes her head at my grandfather.

"Honey, get the car."

My grandparents get me into the car and we go to K-Mart to buy me a dress. My grandmother is holding up dresses to me.

"Now this is going to be your Easter dress too."

Easter, I forgot about the holiday that is coming soon. I started to cry because Sally will not be there to hunt for Easter eggs.

The previous Easter, our cousin Vicky was a baby, and it was a very nice, sunny day. Our grandmother had taken us to church for Easter service at Morgan Road Nazarene Church. I remember Sally and me standing in line with all the other kids just waiting for the Easter Race to start.

"Get on your mark…get set…go!"

Sally and I ran as fast as we could. We got so excited every time we found something. There were Easter eggs, candy, and toys.

Sally had found this pink stuffed Easter bunny holding a colored egg and knowing that Vicky was only a baby she went and gave the pink bunny to her.

My eighth birthday is going to be a few weeks after Easter and I am mad because Sally was not going to be there. My last birthday, Sally was the only person other than my grandparents that cared enough to say "happy birthday" to me; she even made a picture for me in Kinder Kare.

"Nancy how's this dress?" my grandmother asked me bringing me back to the present time.

"Fine."

Really, I did not like it for it was an ugly dress. It is a one piece with the bottom part having an awful flower design and the top which was separated at the waist with peach elastic and had a vest the matched the bottom half.

I ran out of the store as fast as possible.

As I ran out the door crying, others could tell that I was a mess.

I began to scream no words, just screaming.

As my grandmother is paying for the dress, my grandfather comes outside to be with me and he lets me do what I feel like doing to make me feel good. He just stands there to make sure that I do not get hurt.

I sure have cried for many reasons, but this was the worst. People looked at me as if I was a lost little girl, and I felt like I was lost.

My grandmother comes out of the store.

"Come on you two, let's get into the car."

The three of us pulls back into the funeral home's parking lot; grandmother takes me into the bathroom and helps me change into my dress.

I go into the parlor. The room that was empty when I left to go to K-Mart is now beginning to fill up with people.

Aunts, uncles, family friends, and people I did not even know; all of them are looking at me.

"We're sorry, honey."

"Are you okay?"

They are taking pictures, I feel like a freak.

I look up at the front of the parlor room. I see my kindergarten teacher, Mrs. Johnson. David motions to me to come to him.

I slowly walk over to David and Mrs. Johnson, wondering what she is doing here. My parents are mean enough to me. Does she really have to be here too?

I look at David.

"Go with Mrs. Johnson to her car."

"Okay."

Her car is parked in front of the funeral home's front door.

Mrs. Johnson opens the front passenger door of her large white car. While I am standing there next to the car, she looks at me.

"Hold out your arms."

I look into my arms and there are all of Sally's belongings from her class; blue tennis shoes with white laces that look like wet noodles, her bright yellow rain jacket, paintings of a kindergarten artist that belongs on a fridge somewhere and her rainbow colored rug that I passed down to her to use for class naps.

As I hold Sally's things, Mrs. Johnson does not say anything. She just gets into her car and drives off. I just stand there in disbelief. How could she do this and what am I to do now?

I walk into the funeral, feeling somewhat numb. I carry the things that belonged to my sister to my mother and David.

David takes the belongings. Even though I was only seven years old, I knew something was wrong with this.

I was still confused about why Mrs. Johnson came to the funeral and did not even see Sally. Why would she come just to give me Sally's belongings?

Mrs. Johnson lives right next door to us; she could have waited until we got home to bring the belongings over. If she did not want to see us, she could have put the belongings on our porch.

I feel like this was not the time for Mrs. Johnson to upset me, she was so mean to a lot of kids. There was this one time a boy in class had to go to the bathroom bad.

"Mrs. Johnson, I have to go to the bathroom."

"No Tony, you can wait until I am done here."

"No…I really have to go."

"You will wait."

Mrs. Johnson is done talking to the class.

"It is time for a class break."

Tony runs to the bathroom, but ends up at the end of the line. By the time it is his turn, he wet himself. Mrs. Johnson saw what happened and yelled at him.

"Stupid…now you can just sit there in your wet pants until it is time to go home."

He spent the rest of class embarrassed and crying. I sat in my chair thinking how mean that was of Mrs. Johnson to do that to my classmate.

I am standing there next to the casket and off to the side is a small sitting room that I like to go into, to be by myself.

This area has a large opening in the wall to see out of, but others find it hard to look into because of these vertical wooded slats that are angled just so, you can look out and see everything, kind of like a one-way window.

After I handed the belongings over to David, he takes them to the car. I head to the family area, but on the way people with cameras stop me for picture taking; including my parents.

My father Ben Chesebro comes over and sits next to me.

Mother and David did not like Ben because they want Ben out of our lives. When my mother met David, she was still married to my father.

David comes over and stands in front of my father and me.

"You're not allowed in this room…go now."

"I am Nancy's father and I have the right to stay here."

"You have no rights…go sit with the others."

My father goes to Edith, his mother, and Lisa, his sister, next to the casket.

My father is talking to my grandmother and aunt. I cannot hear what is being said, but I can tell my father is upset because he is waving his hands around.

Grandmother and aunt Lisa looks over at me, I am wondering what is going and I walk to the casket to hear.

David comes back with a person that works at the funeral home and points to my father, grandmother, and aunt.

"Sir, you are causing problems. You need to leave the building."

"Nancy is my daughter and I am staying."

"I have nothing to do with family problems; my control is here at the funeral home. Now I need to ask you again to leave or I will have to call the police."

My grandmother takes my father's arm.

"Let's just go."

I am so glad they had to go. I do not mind my grandmother and aunt, but when I am around my father, I feel sick.

I go to sit back in my chair in the small room. I am looking down at the floor, crying.

Sometimes I have an inner voice that talks to me. That inner voice started talking to me now.

"Nancy, look up right now."

I look up and I was surprised because standing there in front of Sally was Mrs. Smith and Mrs. Hency, two teachers from my school along with Mr. Curtis, my principal.

The last time I had seen them was in school just the other day. They were so nice to Sally and me.

I went to school the day after Sally died. I went to the corner to meet Rachael John.

Rachael sees me, but not Sally.

"Where is Sally?"

"Oh, Sally died last night."

We say nothing more and just walk to school.

I get into class and I sit at my desk, this kid, Tommy, starts pulling my hair.

I am so sick of Tommy that I stand up and start yelling.

"Stop it now!"

Tommy starts laughing at me.

I raise my right hand and smack him. He goes to hit me back. I start running around the room and Tommy is chasing me.

Mrs. Smith now notices the two of us are getting into it.

"You two stop it and come here now."

Tommy goes straight to Mrs. Smith, but I refuse to. I just start yelling at Tommy.

"You are just mean and if you tease me again, I will break your nose next time!"

Mrs. Smith is shocked at my behavior. I am not a troublemaker and I do not threaten people.

"Nancy, come here right now."

"Tommy, go sit down and I will talk to you later."

"Now, Nancy what's wrong with you? This is not like you."

I know the kids didn't hear the morning news and I wasn't sure if my teacher did ,but I do know that that morning my parents went next door to tell Mrs. Johnson that Sally wouldn't be in school because she was sick.

Therefore, as I fall into Mrs. Smith's arms, I start to cry.

"My sister died last night."

I think I must have blacked out in her arms because next thing I know, I am in the office, and my mother and David were there.

Principal Curtis tells them.

"You need to take Nancy home and let her rest. Letting her come to school in this condition is not the wisest thing to do."

"But she insisted on going to school."

"You are the adults and should know better."

Mr. Curtis shakes his head and says, "I cannot believe this!"

Mr. Curtis hugs me and says, "Nancy, it is time for you to go home and get some rest."

As I am sitting behind these slanted pieces of wood, I am hoping that Mr. Curtis gives me the same comfort he did that day in his office.

I look around the corner so they could see me; they wave at me and come over.

Mrs. Hency is the first to give me a hug.

"Are you okay?"

"I guess so."

As Mrs. Hency sits next to me, Mrs. Smith hugs me.

"It is okay if people see you cry, crying can help you."

Mr. Curtis hugs me as Mrs. Smith sits on the other side of me.

I am thinking about how nice Mrs. Smith, Mrs. Hency and Mr. Curtis always were to me. Mrs. Smith and Mrs. Hency would keep me after school and just spend time with me doing whatever I wanted and sometimes I would wash the blackboards in both their rooms. Mr. Curtis sometimes sent me home with some clothes or food and a snack to eat on the way home.

Mrs. Smith and Mrs. Hency always knew that I like to write and brought me some paper and pencils to help me.

They go to sit down. I really want them to sit with me, but I am afraid that Mother and David would get upset as they did with Ben.

As I sit sobbing because I want my sister back, I know Mrs. Smith, Mrs. Hency and Mr. Curtis really love and care for me and I really need to know that right now.

I write notes to Sally on the paper my teachers gave me to keep me busy. I am writing, "I love you," "please wake up" and "I'm sorry I did this to you" then I put them next to Sally because I want Sally to know that I am going to miss her.

The funeral director closed the casket.

I start to cry out.

"No…I need her!"

I run to the casket begging.

"Please open it; I don't want you to take her!"

My grandmother Howard comes and takes me by the hand back to my seat.

Hank (my grandfather), Raymond (assistant pastor), Larry (David's brother), and Rodney (family friend) are the pallbearers as they carry the casket. We follow behind and then everyone else follows us.

We get into the family car provided by the funeral home and as we are sitting there waiting to drive off. All I am thinking about are the notes that everyone saw me putting into the casket.

I have at home Dick and Jane books that my speech teacher Mrs. Strand gave me. I would try to teach Sally how to read them and all she wanted to do was look at the pictures.

I am hoping that Sally learned enough to read what I wrote so she will know that I was sorry.

I am standing in front of Sally's grave, listening to the pastor. I cannot believe that Sally was never going to come home again; I lost my sister.

I am spending the night with my grandparents.

I wake up and grandmother is fixing breakfast. After I eat, I go to sit on the sofa. I am looking out the glass of the sliding door at the playground.

My grandfather smiles at me.

"Do you want to go and play?"

"No."

I lay on the sofa and the doorbell rings; it is pastor Gowen and his wife.

Grandfather and the pastor stay in the hall, talking while Mrs. Gowen comes into the living room with grandmother and me.

Mrs.Gowen has a present wrapped in purple wrapping paper in her hands.

"Your birthday is coming up soon and we wanted to give you something early."

Mrs. Gowen puts the gift on my lap.

"You can open it if you like."

I slowly opened it. It was the most beautiful doll I have ever seen. She was an old-fashioned baby doll with pantaloons and the bonnet matched the white dress with purple flowers all over it; I named her Lilac because I love lilacs.

I gave Mrs. Gowen a big hug.

"Thank you!"

It is April 26, 1978, only forty-eight days after Sally died, and it is my birthday. It's David's birthday too.

I am in the living room lying on the cat urine-smelling couch. I have nothing on my mind; sometimes I like to think of nothing because it was as if I did not exist.

From the bedroom, my mother calls me.

"Nancy, come into the bedroom."

I go to the room. Much to my surprise, my mother and David had a birthday present for me. I was so excited; finally, they are giving me something to celebrate my birthday.

David smirks at me as mother hand me a small package.

"Here we got this for you."

I open my present. I am so excited, wondering what it could be.

It is a little black photo album. I open it; it is filled with pictures of Sally lying in her casket. In some, there are pictures of family and friends standing in front of the casket looking at Sally and some people are smiling.

I am confused and look over at my mother and David; my mother looks at me.

"You were the one that got into the nail polish, not Sally, weren't you?"

"What, now you're going to listen to me, now that it's too late? Yes, I did get into the nail polish!"

My mother is now looking over the top of me.

"Don't talk back, you know better."

I am now crying.

"Because you killed Sally, for your punishment, you are to look at these pictures and remember that it's because of you she is dead."

My mother backs away from me and points at the bedroom door.

"Now go put on your purple Sunday dress."

I look up at my mother while I cry.

"Now!" he yells at me.

"Okay."

I put on my favorite dress, for it makes me feel like a princesses when I wear it, but I do not feel like one this time.

I come down the stairs and David is out in the car and my mother at the bottom of the stairs.

"Get into the car."

I grab my white sweater lying on the landing of the stairs.

I get into the car and the next thing I know we are standing at Sally's grave.

Mother looks at me.

"Kneel down."

I look at her confused.

"Your mother said kneel." said David as he pushes me on the ground.

David says to me in a mean voice, "Now pray for forgiveness from your sister."

I looked up at my mother.

"Forgiveness for what?"

She says, "For killing your sister."

I am here kneeling and shivering and it is almost night, I feel like I am going to fall over and my knees are wet with mud from the rain earlier in the day.

I can hardly say the words that my mother tells me to say.

"Say it now and loud so I can hear you!"

I folded my hands and bow my head and say aloud, "I'm sorry I killed you Sally and I should be the one buried there, not you."

I see a quick flash of light; I look up just as my mother was taking a camera from her face.

A few days later, my mother gives me the picture that was taken at Sally's grave.

"Here, put this picture in your black album of Sally's funeral."

Chapter Four

"And He tells me I am His own, and the joy we share as we tarry there, none other has ever known."
~I Come to the Garden Alone by C. Austin Miles~

After the murder of my sister, I was lost. She was my best friend that I could tell everything to and now she was gone.

Sally and I only had each other, we did have our friend Rachael, but she did not know everything. I kept jumping from foster home to foster home for some time, now it was time to add schools to the list too.

Looking back, I remember hating going to different schools all the time, but now as an adult, I realize that by doing so I have become more understanding of all kinds of people. How sad that one had to go through a lot of abuse in order to be more understanding of other people. I could have learned it just as easy from my parents just teaching me and being an example.

In 3rd grade I was told the most wonderful loving words from a person I loved very much, "…just remember there are people who do love you and never want to hurt you."

Wow, what powerful words to tell anyone and they were told to me, the best gift ever.

It is summer; I am out playing with spray bottles with my friends, Paula and Peter, who are brother and sister.

We are having fun chasing and spraying each other, yelling and laughing. I am chasing Peter around the block. As we go around the corner, back on our street, I am running through the grass and I step right on a bee.

As tears are rolling down my face because of the pain, I run into the house.

"Mom, I got stung by a bee"

"You're fine."

"I feel really sick."

"Go get changed, grandma Honey will be here."

I start throwing up; I even throw up blood. My breathing is getting worse and my foot is swelling and I have bumps all over.

Thanks goodness grandmother Honey is here.

I lay there on the sofa feeling dizzy and sick grandmother comes over to me and hugs me.

Grandmother looks over at my mother.

"What is wrong with her?"

With the wave of her hand, Bonnie answers.

"It is nothing. She just got stung by a bee."

"Does this really look like nothing to you?"

Grandmother then looks at David.

"David, take her to my car, we need to get her to the hospital right away."

I think I slept on the way to the hospital because I wake up and I am lying in a hospital bed in a room.

The doctor comes in.

"Nancy, you need to be very careful when playing outside."

"Why?"

"Because you are very allergic to bees. This means that if you get stung, you will get very sick. So it is important to be careful and, if you get stung, make sure to say something so that you can be taken care of right away."

"Okay."

"Now you just rest and you will be back home in a few days."

I am in the 3rd grade and Mrs. Hency is my teacher. When I was in Mrs. Smith's class, Mrs. Hency was not just another teacher for she has always been around. Her daughter lived a few doors down from me on Jericho Road so I got to know Mrs. Hency even before I had her for a teacher.

School had just started a few months ago and I still feel very sad because I am still missing Sally.

Mrs. Hency knows that at times I am missing Sally and need to be alone. She allowed me to go in the back of the room on the gym mats and do whatever I need as long as I did not disrupt the other kids.

I am sad, feeling alone and I really need to cry. I go to the mats with my sweater and I am laying there crying.

"Okay class, get your reading books out, and read the next five pages to yourself."

Mrs. Hency kneels down next to me and she is rubbing my back.

"Oh, Nancy, I am sorry you are so sad, just remember there are people who do love you, and never want to hurt you."

I am walking back to class after lunch and Mrs. Hency has this man talking to her in the room.

"Nancy is depressed and I need to take her to Franklin school."

"Of course she is depressed. She lost her sister in the spring."

"Well, no matter. She needs to go with me. She just may do better in another school and if she doesn't do better, then she will be put in special education."

"This is not right, but it just might come easier if she hears it from me. I can tell you right now she will still be depressed and she doesn't belong in special education just because she is sad."

"Okay, you tell her, but just know that I am just doing my job."

"Just one last thing, tell your boss they are wrong and Nancy should be able to stay at Post school where she knows people for the last thing she needs is to lose the staff here that she has found comfort in and her friends."

I come into the room and the man goes out to the hall. I look at Mrs. Hency.

"Honey, come here."

I look at her with tears in my eyes and slowly walk over to her. I can tell that Mrs. Hency is sad too.

"Honey, that man is here to take you to another school. We think this might help you with your sadness."

"But I don't want to...do I really have to go?"

"Yes, Nancy."

The man comes in to get me.

"Come on Nancy, we have to go now."

I start to cry really hard.

"I...I don't want to."

"Sorry, but you have to."

I turn and look at Mrs. Hency, she grabs me and hugs me real tight.

"I love you Nancy and I am always here for you, remember that."

"I will."

The man and I go out to the hall, standing there is Mrs. Smith and I run to her and hug her tight, hoping that she will be able to help me.

"Mrs. Smith, I don't want to go."

"I know sweetie, but you have to, it just might be nice for you. I am also here for you and you will be in my prayers."

Out of the school with this man I go.

I am so sad and angry, I miss Mrs. Hency and I am always asking for her because I love her and want to be in her class.

No one seems to care so I start acting up.

The class is working quietly at their desk; I am going to yell.

"This class stinks, Mr. Cole stinks, and everyone in this class stinks!"

My classmates laugh and Mr. Cole looks at me.

"Now that is enough, sit back down."

"No...no...no...I don't have to do anything you tell me to do!"

"Nancy, go to the office."

"Good! Now I don't have to stay in this stinking room anymore!"

As I go out the door, I slam it shut.

I am in the fourth grade now; I do not remember much of my summer maybe because I was numb to things.

Except that my mother started to let other men have sex with me and she even had sex with me at the same time the men would. Afterwards, the men would give her money.

My mother told me that I was old enough to look at magazines with naked people in it.

I am sitting on the back of David's car looking at a naked magazine and my friend Paula comes up to me.

"What are you looking at?"

I show her with a smile on my face.

"Where did you get that?"

"My mother, she said that I was old enough to look at these pictures."

Paula does not say anything. She just goes into her house because her mother is calling.

Men keep coming around giving my mother money after they would have sex with me.

Ed Ives was one of the men that was at my house a lot.

Ed had sex a lot with my mother and me at the same time. My mother had moved into my room and I got Sally's room. Ed would go into my mother's room. I would come into my mother's room and Ed would look at me.

"Lay on the bed next to your mother."

I look over at her.

"Everything will be fine and you'll be okay," says my mother.

Slowly, I go to the bed and lay next to my mother and she is naked. Ed, then undressed me as I cry and looked over at my mother, she smiles at me. As soon as Ed has me fully undressed, he lays upon me. Ed puts his privates inside my privates.

"Ouch! That really hurts."

"Don't worry, you will be okay. You'll get used to me and it won't hurt."

Ed is moving on top of me, my mother is starting to kiss me all over. Ed looks at my mother.

"Lie down next to Nancy."

Ed is bending over her playing with his privates. My mother is moving around she puts her fingers inside my privates and Ed is kneeling behind her.

They both get dressed and I am here in the bed. I cry as I watch Ed give money to my mother.

I am hoping that, because of my problems at Franklin school, I will be sent back to Post school.

It is morning and my mother is yelling up the stairs to wake me up for school.

"Nancy, get up and get ready for school. Your bus will be here soon!"

I think to myself, "School bus? But I walk to school."

I come downstairs.

"What do you mean get ready for the bus? I walk to school."

"You're not going to Franklin."

"What do you mean; do I get to go back to Post?"

"No, you are going to go to Roosevelt school. You were causing trouble there so you are going to be in a special class."

"Special?"

"It is called special education. Now get ready."

I have two very nice teachers, Mrs. Vanskicle and Mrs. Greenacres. I am going to be as good as gold because I want to go back to Post when I am in fifth grade.

I am happy here because I really like Mrs. Greenacres. We are going to Clear Lake Camp for a field trip for a few days.

I am waiting in the back of the line to get on the bus because I have a question to ask Mrs. Greenacres.

"Mrs. Greenacres, can I sit with you on the bus?"

"Sure you can, Nancy. I would like that."

On the last day of fourth grade, I get off the bus and go into the house. My mother has boxes packed with our things in them.

"Go to your room and get what you want to take with you."

"Take with me where?"

"We are moving."

"What…why?"

"Both David and I have found someone else and you and I are moving in with John Sweet, my boyfriend."

"David is staying here?"

"Yes…he is dating John's wife, Susan. They are getting a divorce."

I go and get my things and Mr. Sweet puts them into David's car so David can take me to my new home. My new address is on Randolf Street.

Fifth grade is here at Lakeview School and by now, my days just are blurs. Physically, I am here, but not emotionally. The only thing that seemed to hit me was when Carter lost the Presidency to Reagan. Sitting in the library with other kids and teachers, I am crying because I wanted Carter to stay in the White House.

I want to learn more. I want any book that has to do with history. I find that reading is my love and it helps me to escape my "history."

Moving in with my mother's boyfriend John does not stop Ed from coming over. The only thing is that my mother does not have sex with us anymore; it is just Ed and I.

My mother lets Ed take me home with him because his wife is out of town.

My mother tells me, "You're going to go play with his two girls."

I play with the girls until nighttime. Ed sends his girls to bed and tells me that I am sleeping down stairs on the pullout bed.

"Nancy, come into my office with me."

Ed closes the door and he turns on a movie projector and has it playing on a screen right behind me. He sets me on the couch in such a way that I have full view of the screen.

"Now Nancy, don't worry. Everything will be okay. Just do what I tell you to do."

"Okay."

"I want you to watch this movie with me and whatever the woman is doing I want you to do and I will do what the man is doing."

"Okay, I know I have to do what I'm told."

I do not want my mother to get mad at me.

I start to grab and rub his privates the same way the woman on the screen is doing. Next thing the man grabs her hair, pushes her head into his privates, and tells her to put it into her mouth. Ed does the same thing at the same time.

"Do what the woman is doing. I know you know how; you have done it to me before."

He is done with me.

"Keep your clothes off and go to bed."

"But I am cold and want to put my clothes back on."

"You won't be cold. I have enough blankets to keep you warm."

Later, Ed wakes me up when he crawls in bed next to me. He slides under the bedding and he puts his hand on my privates. He rubs me and puts his fingers into my privates. He kisses me on the lips, puts his tongue into my mouth, and moves it around.

Ed then kisses my chest and works his way down to my privates. After kissing me down there, he puts his privates inside of me.

His daughters come down the stairs.

"Go back to bed now."

They go back up stairs, one of them see me crying.

"Are you okay Nancy?"

"She is fine; I am taking care of it. Now go!"

He goes back to moving his body on top of mine. He pulls his privates out of me, he squirts all over my privates as he has done before. He gets up and goes into the kitchen and I put my underwear on. He comes back with a washcloth and hands it to me.

"Here, I will clean you up."

"No, I just want to sleep" and roll over all curled up in a ball.

It is morning, Ed hands me a fistful of money.

"Tell your mother that there's extra for being good and listening to me."

There is a honk in the front yard; it is my mother and her boyfriend John. I run out to the car, jump into the backseat, and hand my mother the money from Ed right in front of John.

"Ed says there's extra because I was a good listener."

John looks at my mother and then me.

"Extra … for what? Why is Ed giving you money for being a good listener?"

John is not the smartest person in the world, but at least he could put two and two together.

My mother looks at him, and then she gives me a dirty look.

"Don't worry, everything is okay."

John looks at me.

"Nancy … why did Ed give you money?"

"He always gives mom money after he has sex with me."

John is mad.

"How could you do that, Bonnie?"

"It is no big deal."

"We are going to the police and you will turn Ed in and if you don't, I will turn both of you in."

The police want my clothes that I am wearing, and I am wearing my favorite brown with big white polka dot skirt, blouse, underwear, and socks. The police take everything, but my shoes. I handed everything to the policewomen.

"Sorry honey, we are not going to be giving these back to you, but you can have these clothes."

I put on the clothes and I am thinking that all I want is my skirt back, not some clothes that are a little too big for me.

Two days after Ed Ives arrest, David calls my mother and tells her that a friend of mine is visiting her aunt who lives two doors down from him on Jericho and that she wants me to come over and spend the night.

With my overnight clothes in hand and a smile on my face I say, "Great" and walk out the door.

I get to Jericho Road and saw Tina; she hugs me. We are so excited to be able to play with each other.

"Where are we sleeping, at your house or at your aunts?"

"I asked for you to come and play, not spend the night, my mother has class in the morning and my aunt isn't going to be around. You are not able to sleep over. Didn't your dad tell you this?"

"No, he said that I could spend the night."

"Sorry."

"That's okay," I say as my heart was sinking, "let's play."

"Hey Tina, do you like it when your dad puts his privates in your mouth?"

She is speechless for a moment.

"My dad doesn't do that."

"Doesn't he touch you in your privates at all?"

Tina seems more shocked. "We don't do those kinds of things in my family. My parents tell me that it's wrong to let others touch me and I shouldn't touch others either."

After the shock wore, off and done playing, I start to walk home. David comes out on his porch.

"Nancy, come here. I have something of Sally's to give to you."

When my mother and I moved, we were not allowed to take anything of Sally's so if he was willing to give me something of hers, you can bet I will go and get it.

I ran up to the porch wondering excitedly what it could be that he wanted to give me.

"Come into the house while I get it."

Slam…click…the door shuts and locks behind me.

"Go into the living room, I'll be right back."

David comes to me with his hands behind his back.

"Take off your clothes."

I look at him confused. "What?"

"If you want anything of Sally's, take off your clothes."

Thinking that he has something for me to keep of Sally's behind his back, I do as I am order.

David pulls his hands from behind his back. He smirks like a fox that has just trapped his dinner in his den. It is a rope and not just any rope. It's a white plastic clothesline rope, the kind that Sally and I got beaten from in the past by him. Therefore, in my mind, I think that he is going to beat me with it and I have no idea why.

I wish that I was going to get a beating, but oh no comma no, he ties me up instead. He not only ties my arms, hands, feet and legs, but he also runs the rope across my private area like a thong.

When he ties my hands together, he leaves a little loop at the top of my hands and puts me, standing, on a chair that he gets from the dining room and puts the loop onto a hook that has been in the ceiling forever which once held a chain hanging lamp.

I am standing on the chair and David starts messing around with me, he not only put his fingers in my vagina, but also other items that would send pain racing through my body.

David is now done with the first part of his torture games. He takes me down and lays me onto the floor. While lying there, David loosens up the rope that is across my vagina, which by now is feeling like it is on fire. He is so turned on that, he needs to relieve himself and does so at my expense and then falls asleep holding me in his arms.

It's morning and I'm still tied up and David decides that he needs to have his way with me one more time before letting me go. When he is done, he unties me and watches me as I dress and walks me to the door.

We get to the door and he gives me a long kiss with his tongue and then says, "Thanks see you again."

I then walk out the door without a single thing of Sally's in hand.

As I walk home, I'm crying not only because of what happened, but also because I was in so much pain that I could hardly walk. The pain lasts for days.

I get back home and go straight to bed without saying a word; I just lay there crying. My mother hears me crying and comes in.

"What's your problem cry baby?"

"Never mind."

"John wants me to find out why you're crying."

Therefore, I tell her what happened with David at Jericho.

She did not seem to care at all. She made me tell John, his mother and their friends what had happened. I tell them, thinking that John would do something about it like he did with the Ed Ives thing, but, much to my surprise, he didn't.

Not long after David hurt me, my mother was reconnected with my uncle Dave, my father's brother, and other family members.

My father's sides of the family are Jehovah's Witnesses so I started to study with my grandmother Edith, Ben's mother.

Dave took me on motorcycle rides; one day he took me to a nearby park and raped me. By this time, I am thinking that it is a normal thing to be raped so I got to the point that I had stopped fighting back.

Dave also knew that I wanted piano lessons and he paid for them as long as I would have sex with him. I got tired of having sex with Dave; he then stopped the lessons.

The reason was one day we took his daughter Dawn back to South Haven. On the way back home I saw a carnival and I so wanted to go.

"Dave, can we go to the carnival?"

"Sure, but first, let's pull over and you take off your clothes."

"No."

I started to cry because I really wanted to go. This is why I lost my piano lessons.

We moved to Upton Ave. I am getting ready for school one day and my mother says to me "light the stove".

"I have never done this before with a lighter, how do I do it?"

"Turn the pilot on, light the lighter and stick it by the pilot and it will light."

I turned on the pilot and started to light it the lighter; it would not light right away so I kept trying to light the lighter until it would light.

I went to put the lighter next to the pilot, I never got near the pilot...boom went a big ball of fire in my face.

My first response was to run and get a wet towel to put on my face. My mother had to go to a neighbor to call for help.

It did not even hurt; the doctor said I was lucky that I had no scares. The only thing is that now that my eyesight is completely back, I have to wear glasses and my eyebrows and lashes were burned off along with half the hair on my head.

I believe that there was an angel watching over me, for I should have felt pain along with having some kind of scars.

I am now ten. I never had a real birthday to mark my day; I just knew that I was another year older. I got a real bad beating outside in the yard because I did not come into the house right away from playing with my friends when my mother called me into the house.

Right there in front of my friends that were sisters, who were also my next-door neighbors, my mother came out with a belt to beat me with it.

The sisters went to get their father.

"Bonnie, stop it or I'll call the cops!"

"Go ahead!"

He just turned around and went back into the house. No cops showed up.

Another year goes by and now I am eleven. My mother wants me to ride my bike to the other side of town to get something from the store. I remember getting just a block from the store and wiping out. I hit my head and, next thing I knew, I woke up looking into the headlights of a car coming right at me and cannot remember a thing. I pulled my bike and myself to the curb.

The car pulled into the driveway. A woman gets out of the car and finds me there on the ground.

"Are you okay?"

"I think so. Where am I?"

"Nancy, you're in the old neighborhood. I will take you back to your new home with your bike."

We pulled up to the house and I do not remember the house. I cannot remember much at all. The lady goes up and knocks on the door and gets my mother to come to the car to get me.

My mother walked me into the house, and asked her boyfriend Roger, "Roger, will you take me to the store?"

"Sure. Nancy, go get your shoes back on."

I go to put my shoes on and I cannot remember my right foot from my left. I am still not sure if I was in the right home for even my mother and Roger seem to be a blur to me. Roger tells me, "go to bed. We are not going if you can't remember anything."

I cannot remember why my mother sent me to the store on the other side of town in the middle of winter…I am guessing it was to get her cigarettes.

I am eleven and my uncle Dave has started to have sex with me again. He gets into the shower with his daughter Dawn and I.

He never touches Dawn in any way, just me.

I asked him, "Why do you not touch Dawn?"

"Because she is my family."

"I too am family."

"You're not his real family."

"What do you mean I am not real family?"

"It's just you're not my daughter."

I am sleeping in bed next to Dawn, I feel my uncle go under the covers, I am thinking that he was going to touch me so I prepared myself for the usual touching and sex, I realize something different this time. Instead of me having privates put into my mouth, he put my privates in his mouth. This has never happened to me before.

I am so confused and frightened; yet I am enjoying a feeling I have never had before.

Up until this point, I never had these kinds of feelings. I thought men were supposed to be the one to feel like this and enjoy it, but now I know I can enjoy sex too.

I want more from my uncle; I cannot wait to spend as many weekends as I could with Dawn so I could have sex with my uncle.

Uncle Dave now has a girlfriend that lives above him. I am so jealous because he spends a lot of time with her and he stops having sex with me no comma until they get into a fight and break up. Therefore, Dave starts having sex with me again.

A few weeks have passed and my mother finds out she has a STD from someone. Instead of telling Roger that she sleeps around, she told him that a friend of theirs, Fred, who is a nice guy, had sex with her while she was sleeping and must have gotten it from him.

Roger, the idiot, believes her, so they beat Fred so badly that there is blood all over the living room, kitchen, and bathroom.

After they beat him, they shove him out the door and my mother comes to me.

"Nancy, you clean the blood while Roger and I go out."

The blood is all over the walls and floors. I am crying because it was an awful thing to watch and now I am cleaning it up.

A year has passed. My mother and I run into him on the street. He has a limp that he never had before. I am listening to him and my mother talk.

"Fred, why are you limping like that?"

"I have been limping like this since you and Roger beat me."

"Did we really hurt you that bad?"

"Yes."

"Sorry."

"That's okay."

"Bye Fred."

"Bye Bonnie."

My mother and I get back home and she notices that Roger has finished the white meat from the chicken that was leftovers from the night before.

My mother yells, picks up a sharp knife, and stabs Roger in the stomach.

"You know all I eat is white meat!"

As she is ramming the knife into Roger, I see blood squirt out like a water gun.

I run out the door with my nightgown on and no shoes in the rain to the gas station to call for help.

The cops get to the house and Roger is lying on the kitchen floor. Roger tells the cops that it was an accident.

Many times in the past, I had to sleep in these streets for school the next day. Well, today is no different. Roger has been home from the hospital for a few days and we are kicked out of 121 Upton Ave because my mother is not paying the rent.

My mother has a male friend that runs a gas station, so he lets us sleep on the floor of the gas station's garage when it closes. There is oil and other gross stuff on the floor.

I am lying there holding my book bag close in fear that it will get lost. After all, it is all I had left and I am making sure that I do not lose my bag. Anything else of mine is gone because mother does not want to carry my things around. All her precious things like drugs and alcohol are all she was willing to carry. I am carrying my own clothes and treasures

Chapter Five

"Born free to follow your heart."
~Born Free-by Don Black~

With age comes freedom. To think my first form of freedom
came at the age of twelve. Oh yes, my voice was finally heard
for the first time. Things were starting to head in the right
direction for me.

At the age of thirteen, a new freedom that I did not want was
thrust upon me. I was upset about this because of the
selfishness of my grandmother, but what could I do for I was
still a kid.

Therefore, I took the good with the bad and soon found out
that the freedom that was thrust at me turned out to be the
best thing that I could have asked for. For within this freedom
I found people who saw me as a caring and deep individual
and showed me that every day.

I saw it as an opportunity of a lifetime, for I was finally away
from all the abusers.

It is my birthday; I am twelve years old, living in Marshall, Michigan. I am walking to see my lawyer and I am thinking about the visit from my social worker a few days ago. She told me that in a week I am being sent back home to my mother. I really do not want this. I reach Mr. Ward's office, walk in his lobby, and smiled at the secretary.

"Hi Nancy, Mr. Ward will be out in a minute."

"Okay, thanks."

After looking at the books on the bookcases built into the wall, I sat down on a reddish brown leather chair. The office is nice with its walnut and cherry wood.

The private office door opens.

"I am ready for you, Nancy."

"Hi Mr. Ward."

"Have a seat, how are you doing?"

"Okay. My social worker saw me the other day."

"How did the visit go?"

"She told me that the state is going to send me back to my mother."

"How do you feel about that?"

"I can't take this anymore. I do not want to be with my mother."

"Nancy, you know because you are twelve, you can take your mother to court and sue for her rights to be taken away, that is, if you have someone to live with."

"Yes, I want to do that."

"Do you have someone that would take you in and let you live with them?"

"My aunt Lisa, my father's sister, might take me. We get along very well and I will see her in a few days."

"You talk to her and give her my business card to call me if she is interested in having you."

Two days after my visit with Mr. Ward, I go to spend time with my aunt Lisa.

"Aunt Lisa, I have something to ask you."

"What is it?"

"I talked to Mr. Ward and he told me that, because I am now twelve, I can take my mother to court and have her rights taken away, but there is a catch."

"What is that?"

"I need someone that is willing to let me live with them. I need a place to go. I was wondering if I could live with you."

"Do you really want to live with me?"

"Yes I do. Mr. Ward said to give you his card if you are interested and to call him."

"If that is what you really want, then yes, you can live with me. Give me his card and I will call him."

My aunt called Mr. Ward right away.

"Mr. Ward please…Mr. Ward, this is Lisa Davis, Nancy's aunt. Yes, Nancy, told me that…Okay, I will tell her. Thank you, bye."

"Okay Nancy, everything is now in motion. You still need to leave the foster home in Marshall, so the state is going to find one here in Battle Creek for you to stay at until all the court stuff is done."

I went up to Aunt Lisa, put my arms around her, and gave her a big hug.

"Thank you so much, Aunt Lisa. I also know a foster home I was in a long time ago that I would like to stay at."

"Where is that?"

"I don't know the address, but I can show it to you. I showed it to my mother one day and I told her that I wanted to go back there again someday."

Aunt Lisa and I went for a drive and I showed her the home.

"There it is, that is the last foster home I was in with Sally before she died."

We went back to Aunt Lisa's and she got a hold of the right people and told them of the home.

A week later, I was back at the foster home of Mr. and Mrs. Black. My social worker knocks on the door, Mrs. Black answers.

"Nancy, my, have you grown. I am surprised and happy to know that you remember us for you were really small."

She hugs me.

"Come in."

It did not take me long to settle in, it is as if I was at home again.

"I remember Sally and I being here together," I tell Mrs. Black as she helps me up the stairs and back into my old room that I once shared with Sally.

Two weeks has gone by fast. I guess my mother remembered me pointing out the foster home to her. I went to bed and as I am looking over at the bed Sally once slept in, I had this feeling to cover my head. As I pulled the blanket over my head, I see what looks like glitter flying around my head. I scream and the next thing I know my foster parents and foster sister are standing at my door.

I hear my foster father's voice, "Nancy, don't move."

Next thing I know, my foster father picks me up from my bed and carries me to the hall. As I look behind him, I see the glass all over my bed and the curtains are blowing.

My foster sister calls the police. As my foster father puts me down, I grab the hand of my foster mother; he goes outside to check things out.

The police come and look around the bedroom.

"Did anyone see anything out of the ordinary just before the rock came through the window?"

I am standing there listening to my twenty year old foster sister describe what she saw when she got home.

"I pulled my motorcycle into the driveway and as I parked it, I saw this guy walking down the street."

"Yes, go on."

"I came into the house and I looked out the picture window and I see him standing at the corner under the street lamp, looking at the house."

"Can you describe him?"

"Yes, a husky man with red curly hair, and a red mustache."

As I cry, I yell out.

"It's Roger, my mother's boyfriend. She told him where I am, and he did this."

The report is done, the police leave, and I have to go back to bed for in the morning I have court.

As I am lying next to the window in my foster sister's bed, I am too scared to sleep. I am not sleeping and now I am scared of windows.

It is morning. I crawl out of bed and go straight to the bathroom. As I walk, something does not feel right. I feel like I have glue in my underwear. I pull my pajama bottoms and underwear down. There, sitting in my underwear, was blood. Figures not only do I get the life scared out of me during the night, but I also get to move into womanhood, lucky me, and I have to be in court in a few hours.

My social worker is here to pick me up. As I am walking down the stairs, I hear my foster mother tell her all about what happened last night including the moving into womanhood for me. My social worker sees me on the stairs.

"How exciting for you, now remember to bring some pads with you."

We are at the courthouse. As I walk down the hall, I see my aunt, my grandmother, and my father. I stare at my father because I do not want him there.

I run to my aunt and hug her as I cry.

"What's wrong, are you scared?" She pushes my bangs from my eyes, as my social worker walks up to us.

"She just had a rough night. Someone threw a rock into her bedroom window last night as she was sleeping."

I look up at my aunt, "I know it was Roger."

"But Nancy does have some good news. Tell your aunt the good news about you."

I walk away from the group and mumble, "No, it is not good news."

My social worker leans over to my aunt, grandmother, and father.

"She started her period for the first time in the middle of the night."

My aunt comes over and hugs me.

"You'll be okay."

I am sitting in a chair in the hall, waiting to go into the courtroom. I am thinking to myself, "Finally my side will be heard, and I can get away from my mother."

My lawyer comes out and walks up to us.

"Nancy, come here. We have to talk before going in the courtroom."

"Okay."

"Bonnie has decided to sign her rights away, so that means you don't have to get on the stand, but we do need to go in and listen to the judge make it official."

Everybody is relieved but me.

"Why did she do that?"

My lawyer looked at me.

"I guess Bonnie knows she has been beaten. You're not her meal ticket anymore."

I am upset because I want to have my say to my mother and this was supposed to be my chance to tell her that she's a horrible mother and a poor excuse for a human, that she was my mother and she should have taken care of me even if that means that she goes without.

We all go into the courtroom. Mr. Ward has me sit next to him at the table along with my father. I cannot stand being close to my father and do not want him sitting next to me.

"Mr. Ward, I don't want my father sitting here with us."

"He has the right, for he still has his rights."

Now this takes me by surprise because my mother always told me that he had no rights.

"What do you mean? He has never had rights."

"Your father has always had his rights."

"Well, I want his rights taken away too."

"Not today, Nancy. We need to finish this."

At this time, the judge enters the courtroom and sits in his chair.

"Mr. Ward, have you explained to Ms. Chesebro what is going on here?"

"Yes, your honor."

"Ms. Chesebro, do you understand that your mother is giving up her rights?"

"Yes, sir."

"That means that she has no rights to make any decisions for you."

"Yes, sir."

"This also means that she has no legal obligations to do anything for you."

"I understand, your honor."

"Okay Ms. Chesebro, I will put in the judgment that your mother has given up her rights."

"Thank you, your honor."

It is my thirteenth birthday, but being that my aunt is a Jehovah's Witness, there is no celebration, which is no big deal because my birthday has always been just another day.

I love my aunt very much, but I am not used to answering to someone and she is used to having kids in her house that knew how to be a kid. As for me, I never had the chance to be a kid.

I learned a lot from my aunt, but the stress level is too high because we could not compromise. So now, I have two choices: living with my grandmother or moving to Lowell to a residential home for abused children called Riverview, but that control is now in my grandmother's hands.

Therefore, I go and ask my grandmother if I could live with her, knowing that my father also needed a place to live and I do know that my father and I are not allowed to be living in the same house. This does not bother me for I do not want to live with him

"No, your father needs a place to live and I'm moving him into the house."

"Please change your mind!"

"No, I will choose your father over you any day."

"But he is forty-eight and I am thirteen and need more than he does."

"I have made my decision."

I am going to Marne to a foster family that is within the system of Riverview for there is no bed for me at Riverview right away.

Riverview foster homes are different for these homes are for the Riverview kids and there is only two ways to get into one of these homes. One is, if you are new and there is no room at the Riverview home, you stay there until a bed opens up. The other way is by earning visits by working on your goals in therapy at Riverview and if you were making good progress, you would be placed there, as part of the family and you will be still working on your therapy, only doing so in a foster home.

I really like this foster home. There is the mother and father and they have a son and a daughter of their own. The son and I are the same age and the daughter is one and a half years younger than I am.

A month has passed. I am sent to Riverview where I now have a bed. All that is on my mind on the ride to the home is working hard to go back to Marne to live.

We pull into the large driveway and there is kids playing basketball along with a staff member. This black girl runs up to me and hugs me.

"You must be Nancy; I'm your roommate Brianna…welcome!"

I smiled and hugged her back.

"Who is that worker?"

"That's Mr. Scott."

She pulls me into the group of sweaty kids. Mr. Scott, now I knew this is the man I wanted to marry. Tall, skinny, medium brown hair and his smile, oh my, his smile made everything okay.

"Hi Nancy, I am Mr. Scott and you will be in our group today."

"Hi, nice to meet you."

"Do you like to play basketball?"

"Yes I do."

"Well, Brianna will help you get your things to your room. Then you come back and play."

"Okay."

I had been at the Riverview home for almost a month, it is the first day of school, and I am so excited because I am now in ninth grade, high school. The bus turns into the middle school to drop off kids, everyone gets off, but me.

"Hey there, what's your name?" Says, the driver.

"Nancy."

"Nancy, this is where you get off."

"Oh, no I am in high school."

"No, this bus is only for the middle school. I do not go to the high school."

"Well, something is wrong. I don't belong here."

"I have to drop you off here. When you get in, go to the office, and tell them and they will figure this out for you."

I get off the bus and am so confused. I walk into the school and find my way to the office. At the counter, I feel like I am going to throw up because I do not know what is going to happen. The secretary hangs up the phone and looks at me.

"What can I do for you, hon?"

"I am supposed to be at the high school, but I was told that I need to be here. I need to get this taken care of."

"Okay, what is your full name?"

"Nancy Marie Chesebro."

"How do you spell the last name?"

"C-h-e-s-e-b-r-o"

"Okay, let me check this out."

As I stand there and wait, I start to cry because I have the feeling something isn't going to go right.

"Nancy, our records show that you belong here. Here is your class schedule."

"No! This is not right, something is wrong."

"Do you want to talk to the principal? Maybe he can help you figure this out."

"Yes, please."

As the secretary goes to get Mr. LaSalle, I start to cry even harder and I am thinking to myself, "What is going on here?"

"Nancy?"

"Yes."

"Hi, I am Mr. LaSalle; I understand there is a problem, which you think you should be at the high school?"

"Yes sir. I was in eighth grade last year and I got passing grades."

"Okay Nancy, give me a few minutes to make some calls and then I will have answers for you. Have a seat."

I sit and wait for about ten minutes.

"Nancy, come into my office so we can talk in private."

I go in and sit in the chair in front of his desk.

"Okay, here is what I have found out. You are right, you did have passing grades."

"See, I told you I don't belong here."

"Just wait, there is more. Michigan has this law that, even though you have the grades, you still cannot go to ninth grade."

"What? Why? This doesn't make sense."

"Let me finish. See, this law says that a student has to be in school so many days out of the year. If the student is not, then they have to repeat that grade no matter if they have passing grades or not."

"That is not fair, I like school, and it is not my fault that I wasn't in school all those days because I moved a lot and so I missed school."

"I understand Nancy, but I have to go by the law. I am sorry."

I get my classes and start my first day of eighth grade – again.

It has been a few months since school started and things are not very bad for I have great teachers. Mr. Ackers for history, Mr. Latva for English, Mr. Stien for science, Mr. King for choir and Mrs. Lambert for art. Each one of these teachers makes school fun. It was worth taking the eighth grade again just to have them for my teachers.

My parents never did anything for my birthdays as a young child. Honestly, I do not remember any of my birthdays, but Sally always had one along with the cake and ice cream. Not many seemed to take my birthday to heart for some reason.

Mrs. Lambert's birthday is March 26th and mine is April 26th. I made her a card. Mrs. Lambert was impressed that I knew when her birthday was and that I remembered it. Therefore, Mrs. Lambert remembers mine too.

In class, Mrs. Lambert asked me to spend my lunch with her in her classroom and I agreed to.

When it is lunch, I walk into the art room with my lunch tray in hand. I set the tray down and Mrs. Lambert tells me to close my eyes. I do and I hear the rustling of a paper bag like the rustling of the fall leaves on the ground.

"Open your eyes."

I open my eyes to see the she got me a little light tan stuffed puppy made from the Russ Company.

"I kept hearing this cute guy telling me to buy him for Nancy because it would make her very happy."

She hands the puppy to me.

"Thank you Mrs. Lambert."

"Nancy, I just want you to be happy and I hope this helps."

She then hugged me and I cried because I now know that someone really does care for me enough to remember me on my birthday.

I feel for the first time, that the day I was born is a very important day!

I have made my goals; I get to move back to Marne. I am very attached to Joanne, the mother, and she really is attached to me as a second daughter. Her birth daughter is a bit jealous because I am a good kid and I do not argue back. I just do as I am told to do.

Now, in defense of the daughter, after all, I am an outsider that has come in to be the perfect child, so she thinks. The truth of the matter is that I have learned the hard way to do as you are told.

By no means, does Joanne love me more and she proved this to her daughter by sitting with me to have a sincere talk.

"Nancy, I need you to know that I love you, but I love my daughter too, for she is mine, and she's having problems with you here because she thinks I love you more and I can't allow her to think that."

She reaches out to me to hug me.

"I am her mother first and she means the world to me, but you'll always be in my heart."

I cried.

"I understand."

The truth is I did really understand. I thought, "WOW…that's a mother for you, for a mother takes care of their young at all cost." She taught me a lesson, "That nothing or no one is as important to you and shouldn't be than your own child". I admire Joanne for having such courage.

I go back to Riverview, until another family is found.

Chapter Six

"Now click your heels together three times and say there's no place like home." ~ The Wizard Of Oz ~

I have been in one foster home after another; I have learned not to get attached because it never lasts. This has caused me to have issues. As I got older, I would get close to others, but also keep a wall up. I have learned to enjoy my relationships for the immediate moments and never to expect a future.

It has not taken too long to get another foster home since the reason for me to return to the Riverview home was out of my control. The staff did not want me there long because I belong in a foster home. So now, I am living with the VanLoos. It was not perfect but, on the other hand, it was not bad either. After all, I am fifteen and I know how to take care of myself. I have been doing it my whole life.

I just got done with spring break and I am walking home from the school bus. I look up the street to my house and I see my grandparent's car in front of the house. Why are they here? No one told me they were coming for a visit.

I walk into the house to see them sitting at the kitchen table with my foster mother. My grandmother is talking up a storm; my grandfather is, as always, sitting there quietly for he is a man of few words. I look at my grandmother and she hugs me.

"Nancy Marie…"

Oh no, something is wrong. She only calls me Nancy Marie when something is wrong.

"Can we please go to your bedroom? We need to talk."

"Okay, it is down the end of the hall."

We sit on the bed and she holds my hand.

"Your great-grandmother has died."

I cry and ask "When?"

"Two weeks ago."

"When is the funeral? I want to go."

"We already had the funeral."

"So I don't get to go…that is not fair."

"I am sorry Nancy; we just weren't able to get here until now to even tell you. You are an hour and a half away from my house."

"Go get out…NOW!"

I lay in my bed crying.

My great grandmother Boyer was something for she taught me family secrets to cooking and baking. She would also give Sally and I rides in her wheelchair when we sat on her lap. Visiting her was one of the few great things I did as a child.

I decided to stop studying with the Jehovah's Witnesses because of the brainwashing and the nightmares.

They played on my fears, in order to draw me in. They told me that my sister would never live forever with our Lord and that I was the only one that could bring her through.

Now that I am leaving, they tell me that I will never see Sally again.

There is this Jehovah's Witnesses couple by the name of Phyllis and Paul. I love them very much for they treat me as if I was their child; I am going to get a visit from Phyllis.

Phyllis drives up to the house and I get into the car and give her a big hug. I am giving her the news that I am not going to be a Jehovah's Witness, I think that she will be okay with it for she loves me.

"Hi, Phyllis."

"Hi, sweetie. Where would you like to eat?"

"I don't care, you pick and surprise me."

We get to Pizza Hut, sit down, and started talking as we ate.

" Phyllis, I have something to tell you."

"What is that?"

"I am not going to be a Jehovah's Witness anymore."

"Why?"

"I don't like it and I do not agree with the teachings."

"Time to take you back home."

"I thought we were going to spend the whole day together."

"Well, if you're leaving the Jehovah's Witnesses, then I cannot have anything more to do with you. So, are you sure you want to leave the church?"

"Yes I am."

"Then let's go."

We pull up to the house and Phyllis refuses to hug me or even say goodbye to me. I go into the house, straight to my room and cry. I hear my foster mother come down the hall and into my room.

"Why are you back early?"

"We just decided not to spend the whole day together. Phyllis is upset with me."

"Why is she upset?"

"I told her that I wasn't going to be a Jehovah's Witnesses anymore and because of that she wants nothing to do with me."

"Oh, I see. I will leave you alone."

The VanLoos are getting worn out taking in foster kids so they decide to get out of it. I am going to be going back to Riverview, this time I have requested not to send me to visits, that I will just stay there until I graduate. The staff agrees and now that makes me the oldest at Riverview.

My housemate Carol is being dropped off by Mike and Dianne Nawrocki. Her family she visits on the weekends. Dianne saw me sitting on the sofa, reading. She looks at me, smiles, and I smiled back at her.

It is time for my meeting with Mr. Chuck, my counselor.

"Nancy, the Nawrockis really want to get to know you, would you please consider giving them a chance?"

"I am really not interested in trying another family. I have been in and out of homes so much that I just don't want to deal with another."

"I know Nancy, but this family is really interested in you. Just go for one weekend and see."

"Okay, but there are no promises."

After a few weekend visits with Mike and Dianne, I decide to move in with the family, so it's packing up my things and off to a new home I go.

I am doing things differently, for Dianne has two daughters and I have learned not to get too attached. When I would start to get attached, I not only pulled away I would also do something to get into trouble in hopes that Dianne wouldn't get to close to me. After all, I could not allow her daughters to feel like I am trying to take their mother away.

My counselor has changed to Mr. Eric. I have had him before and from experience, I knew I did not like the idea of having him. Last meeting I had with him, he told me, "Nancy, you should just face it. You're going to be a whore just like your mother and on drugs."

"You have no right to say that and have no idea what you're saying. I am not even interested in having sex."

Well, now he is at Dianne's home to see me and he was not very kind at all.

"Your sister's death is your fault and her death was a dream comes true for you."

"You're crazy!"

I leave my bedroom, which is where we would talk when he came over.

"Get back in here."

"No!"

By this time, Dianne came to see what all the noise is about. I told her what Mr. Eric had said to me.

"Tell her to get into her room, so I can finish her session."

Dianne looks at him, "Your session is done…Nancy doesn't need to go to her room."

"She is being disrespectful to me and she needs to be grounded for two weeks"

"I'm not grounding her, for you are not only being disrespectful to Nancy, but also very mean."

"Dianne, you know I can pull her from your home and not only that I also will revoke your foster care license."

"That's not right."

"Try me, Dianne."

"Nancy, just cooperate and go back to your room and finish your session and keep the peace."

She then assured Mr. Eric that I would be grounded.

The session is done; Mr. Eric did all the talking in which I just spaced out. The only thing I remember him saying to me is, "Nancy, you had better not make me look like a fool again or I'll make sure that you're taken out of Dianne's home."

Mr. Eric and his big power trip walk out the door and as he gets into the car, Dianne looks at me and hugs me.

"Don't worry Nancy. After all, who does he think he is, Superman? You're not grounded."

I smiled and went to my room, not because I was grounded, but because I needed to get rid of some baggage.

I get the album of death that my mother and David had given me for my eighth birthday, for I am starting to take control of my life. I am struggling on the other hand for I feel as though I do not have the right for such control because Sally did, after all, die while taking a punishment for something I did.

After struggling, I decide to take the control as I start to tear those pictures into tiny little pieces. As I tear up ten years of guilt and anger that built up in my soul, I start to feel more and freer with each picture. Not just the anger for Bonnie and David and all the others who have wronged me, but also the anger I had for myself because I feel as though I allowed these things to happen to me.

Then I said to myself, "I know that God placed into my heart not only the emotional strength I needed to tear these pictures, but also the strength to live life and show others. No matter what you have done to me, I am a survivor."

Dianne comes into my room to see how I am doing and saw me sitting on the floor tearing the pictures. Dianne looks at me and says nothing; she just smiles at me and leaves me to be alone with my tearing.

I place the torn pieces into a pile on the floor. I lay next to what once was pictures of guilt and now is a pile of guilt. I lie there crying my heart out. I cried myself to sleep. I wake up with a blanket on me that Dianne had covered me with; it is morning and time for me to get ready for school.

I am going to school with fewer burdens than I have ever had. As I sit here on the bus, I think to myself, "Wow, I really do have control. I don't have to concede to others MY control."

Now, I understand the sweet rewards of having control of my own life.

Chapter Seven

"When the world never seems to be living up to your dreams, it's time you started finding out, what everything is all about." ~Facts Of Life-by Alan Thicke~

With age come new responsibilities. Becoming a senior in high school brought on more than your average teen, whatever "average" is. I have grown and learned a lot; now looking back it was the best thing. Mmmm, you know I would not change a thing.

It is the summer of 1988, I had moved out of my foster home into what is call "Independent Living." Riverview, the State and my foster parents thought I would benefit better, for I can now only answer to myself. Answering to parent figures does not fit me well, just like how it was the with my aunt Lisa when I was thirteen. I did not like it at first but, now that I had been out on my own for a month, I got a job at JcPenney's in coats, dresses, and doing my own thing. I am enjoying this new freedom.

I am hanging out with my good friends and we like to go to a dance club called Top Of The Rock.

I walk into the club. There, hovering over the crowd, is a tall handsome man. I look at him and he smiles. Wow, I have to meet him. I need to ask him to dance.

The night is coming to an end and I still haven't gotten the nerve to ask him to dance. I made sure I stayed in his sights all night in hopes that he will ask me to dance.

The club manager has just announced the half hour call. It is time for me to grab the bull by the horns and ask him myself.

"Hi, would you like to dance?"

"Sure."

Whew, I asked and he said yes and now we are dancing a slow dance. I look up at the 6' 5" handsome guy.

"What grade are you in?"

"I am a senior."

"Me too."

"I am a senior at U of M."

"Oh, I am a senior at East Kentwood High School."

Manager calls last dance.

"Hey Paul, did you drive your own car here?"

"No, I came with my friend Don in his car."

"Would you like me to take you home?"

"Sure, I will tell Don I have another ride home."

We get into my car and I say...

"Let's go for a ride."

As I am driving to Fallsburg Park in Lowell, we are talking and laughing. I pull into the driveway of a friend of mine and it is 1:30 in the morning. Dogs start barking like crazy and I am confused because I know my friend has no dogs, but it has been a year since I have seen him so maybe he has moved.

I decide to back out of the long drive only to go into the ditch on the passenger side. The car is on its side and the only way out is through the driver's side window. I get out first and as I wait for Paul to get out, I look around and the dogs are still barking. As I look over in a big clearing in the park, I start to get worried and start saying in a loud tone, "look, there is a bear."

"No, that is not a bear."

"Yes it is."

We stand in silence for a few seconds, and then the silence was broken.
"Moo."

I burst out laughing. I am laughing because I think it is so funny that I meet this hot man, we get into a ditch together and then I am seeing things. This is something that belongs on a sitcom and I can tell that Paul does not think this is funny, but I cannot help but to laugh.

The barking has woken up the people in the house; they turn on the porch light to see what the commotion is all about. A man comes out on the porch, stops the dogs from the barking, and walks up to us.

"What is wrong?"

"I got stuck in the ditch."

"I will get my truck and chain and I will have you out of there."

"Okay, thank you. I am sorry about waking you."

"That's okay; let's just get you out of there."

We get out of the ditch and Paul and I walk in the dark around the park. We drive over to the baseball field, park, and went to sleep in each other's arms. We wake up and I take Paul to his dad's house.

As Paul is directing me to his dad's, I realize I know the area, but I say nothing. I just take the turns as he tells me to.

"Pull into this driveway."

I pull into the horseshoe driveway; I go all the way through back onto the street.

"No, Nancy, stop. This is where I need to be dropped off."

"Your dad lives here?"

"Yes."

"Are you sure?"

He laughs, "Of course I am sure."

"Wow, which is something. The last foster home I was in, her uncle owns this house."

Now this is an old large farmhouse on acres of an apple orchard with a huge pull barn. This house has twelve bedrooms. I had some great Christmases in this house.

"Well, the guy who owned it has passed away."

"I did not know that."

"Yes, now the kids own it and they don't want to live in it."

"How did your dad and step-mom come to be in it?"

"My dad answered a rental ad, the kids were happy to rent it to him because he is a manager at Ace Hardware, so they have a special agreement for the rent."

"Wow, this is something."

"Well, I guess I don't have to give you the grand tour, now do I?"

"Oh, not at all, for I am sure I could show you a few things out here."

Well, summer break is over and Paul leaves for U of M the following day and I am going to his dads to help him pack.

We are now officially a couple. I am at Paul's and everyone is in bed; we go to his room and we pack. It is now really late and I am sleepy. Paul goes into his bathroom to pack things in there, I lay on the bed to rest my eyes and I must have fallen asleep for Paul is waking me with kisses.

"Good morning, Nancy. We will be leaving soon."

"Okay, I am going out to the car to get my things to get ready."

I leave the bedroom and walk through the kitchen; Paul's dad is there making morning coffee.

"Good morning Bill."

"Good morning."

I go out the kitchen door as Bill's mouth is hanging open for he did not know I was there and to top it off Paul has never had a girl stay over before – his family had never meant any of Paul's female 'friends' until now.

I get ready as Paul is in the kitchen telling his dad that I am riding along.

A week has passed and now it is time for me to start my senior year of high school. I meet up with old friends and we catch each other up on the happenings of the summer.

"So, Nancy … anything new for you?"

"I have a boyfriend."

"Really, you have a boyfriend? Never thought you would be serious about having a boyfriend. You seem to like books better."

"Not true, I like boys just as much. It is just the right one has not come along until now."

"Who is he?"

"No one you know. He is a senior at U of M."

"Oh, do tell."

"Paul Spaulding, he went to Grandville High School."

"That is so cool."

I walk away smiling to myself because I know that they envied me for I have what every high school girl wants – a college boyfriend, a senior to boot.

It is March, spring break and Paul comes to my house.
"Nancy, I need to talk to you."

"Sure, come in. My roommates are gone and I have the whole place to myself."

"I joined the Navy."

"Wow, that's great."

"Yeah, but I need to tell you that we can't see each other anymore."

"What, why?"

"It is hard in the Navy for girlfriends and wives. It just is not fair to ask you, not just wait for me, but to put up with the crap."

So without any further conversation he hugs me, says sorry, and walks out the door.

Three weeks has now passed and I have moved on, so much so I am now dating my good friend Jeremy. Jeremy and I have a lot in common and the biggest thing is our love of history especially the Civil War. Jeremy introduces me to Civil War re-enactments; I so love this for I also met this wonderful couple Bob and Arlene.

I really like Bob and Arlene and I am now close to Arlene, so much so that I refer to her as my mother and Bob, my father.

It is the summer of 1989 and I am a live-in nanny for two boys. Jeremy and I have decided on a mutual break-up, thank goodness it has not affected our friendship for he is really a great guy and I am so happy to still call him a friend.

I get in touch by phone will Bill, Paul's father.

"Hi, Bill, it is Nancy---Nancy Chesebro, Paul's old girlfriend."

"Yes, Nancy, I remember who you are."

"I was just wondering if you will give Paul a message for me."

"Sure, what is that?'

"Give him my phone number and say I would like to hear from him."

"I will do that."

"Thanks, bye."

Ten minutes have passed and the phone rings.

"Hello."

"Hi, Nancy, it is Paul."

"Wow, I just hung up the phone from your dad. You are fast."

"A few months back, when I was back in Grand Rapids, I went to your place and a roommate said you don't live there anymore."

"Do you have a red firebird?"

"Yes."

"That was you, my roommate told me a tall guy with a red firebird stopped by looking for me. I said I have no idea who it is and never gave it another thought. Now I know it was you."

"Yes, I wanted to see you, to find out if you were seeing anyone. If not, then maybe we could give it another try."

"Well, I am not seeing anyone. Do you still want to give it another try?"

"Yes, if you do."

"I do want to."

"I will be moving to Saratoga Springs, New York in a few weeks."

"Wow, that's neat."

It is morning and I give the boy's father my two weeks, explain that I am moving in with Paul. He thinks it is a mistake, but I really want this and am going to do it.

The two weeks seemed to have gone so slow. Paul went to New York before coming to get me to find a place. It is midnight and the phone rings.

"Hi, Nancy, got a place for us. I will be getting you in a few days."

"Okay, I am really looking forward to it."

"Me too."

"Oh, I can't wait."

"Hell, I am leaving now, I want to see you ASAP."

"Okay, bye."

"See you soon."

Wow, it is about seven hours later and Paul has pulled up in the driveway. We greet each other with a hug and kiss, get some sleep and then go meet some family members of Paul's and we head to Saratoga Springs.

We live here in Saratoga Springs together for almost a year and Paul is transferred to Connecticut, since he will only be there for four months, I will stay in New York.

On Easter of 1991, I decide to go to a church I have never been to. As I sit here enjoying the service, my attention is on this very lovely lady with long black beautiful hair. She looks over at me and sees me looking at her, and we exchange smiles. After the service, we greet each other.
"Hi, I am Elaine."

"I am Nancy."

"This is my first time here."

"Mine too, I only came because it is Easter."

"Me too."

"Do you live near the church?"

"No, my boyfriend does. I live in New York City."

"Oh, that's nice, never been there. I have lived here for almost a
year, but I may be moving soon for my boyfriend is in the Navy."

"Do you work here?"

"Yes, I was a nanny back at home and found a part time nanny job
here for a wonderful family."

"Well I will be here for a few more days, would you like to come
over for lunch tomorrow while my boyfriend is at work? We could
get to know each other even more."

"Sure, I would love to."

I go to sleep with excitement that I met someone from New York
City. I get up take a shower and get ready for lunch with Elaine.

I walk fast to my lunch date; I get to the house and knock. Elaine
answers the door with her warm and welcoming smile.

"Hi Nancy."

"Hi."

"Come on in, have a seat. Do you drink tea?"

"Oh yes, I like tea without sweetener."

We set talking up a storm, at one point she asks…

"Are there any famous people you like?"

"Oh yes, I am a big fan of Lucille Ball's and Patty Duke's."

"Really?"

"Yes."

So I proceed to tell her all the facts I know of Lucille and Patty. Elaine says nothing and just listens. It is getting late in the afternoon and her boyfriend will be home soon so I need to get home myself.

April 26, 1991; it is my 21st birthday today and I am going out with friends to celebrate. We go to a bar for a few drinks, laughs, and food. I get back home; it is late so I go to take a relaxing bath. I take the cordless phone into the bathroom with me in case Paul calls. Paul does not call, but Elaine calls me.

"Happy birthday."

"Thank you."

" I have a surprise for you."

"Aw, you didn't have to do that."

" I am sending you train tickets to come into the city for a week with me."

"Wow, that is great…thank you!"

"Oh, there is a second surprise for you. I was going to wait until you got here to tell you, but I just can't wait.'

"Wow, coming to New York City is enough."

"Well, since Lucille Ball has passed, I thought I would do the second best thing."

I say to her, "Yes, I remembered when she passed for she died on my nineteenth birthday."

"Yes, so how would you like to meet Lucille Arnaz?"

"What!? I would love to."

"See, Lucille Ball, and Lucille Arnaz are my aunts by marriage."

"Really? Now I feel like a fool sitting and telling you all those facts and here you knew it and then some."

"Yes, really. See, my uncle is Laurence Luckinbill who is married to Lucille Arnaz."

"Wow, he played Spock's half-brother, Vulcan Sybok in Star Trek V: The Final Frontier ."

So she gives me traveling information and hangs up. I then lay back in the tub thinking of how as a young child my sister and I loved watching, "The I Love Lucy Show" and how I was watching the show the night my sister died.

I get to New York City; I meet Lucille, Bill and their son in the "Rainbow Room" on the 65th floor of the "Rockefeller Plaza" and eat the best Caesar salad ever.

Paul is stationed in Norfolk, Virginia, but we are going to be living in Virginia Beach. We have not been here long and now I am pregnant so when I am about two months along, on November 2, 1991, we will be married.

Chapter Eight

**"Walk on, walk on, with hope in your heart, and you'll
never walk alone."**
~You'll never walk alone-by Rodgers and Hammerstein~

Motherhood, I now get to be the mother that I never had. This
scares me for I have no idea what a good mother really is. Oh,
I have had many women in my life that has been very kind to
me, but that is so different then a mother twenty-four/seven.
Nothing I can do but my best, for I am going to have a little
soul that is going to depend on me and someday I hope will
look up at me in spite of all the mistakes. Even though not
planned, the little soul is ever so wanted.

It is May 2, 1992; I am in the bathroom getting ready to go out to breakfast with Paul. I lift my arms into the air and I feel a leak down there that I just knew was not urine.

"Paul!"

"What?"

"I am pretty sure that my water just broke."

"But you're not due for another eight weeks."

"Well, I guess the baby doesn't know that. Damn and I am hungry."

We get the things I need for the hospital and call the doctor. We get to the hospital, the nurse is checking to see if my water really has broke and it has.

May 3rd at 7 am, almost twenty-four hours later, 5lbs 12ozs and 21 inches long, Angela Marie Spaulding is born. She is so beautiful; she has lots of dark curly hair and a tiny little head.

On May 4^{th,} Angela and I are going home. I sleep when she sleeps. The following morning, Angela seems to be sleepy, she eats very little. Paul comes home from working on the submarine and sits on the sofa; I bring Angela to him to hold and to take a picture. As I step back to take the picture, I notice because of having her in different lighting that she is looking yellow. I snap a few pictures and then look at her again.

"Paul, doesn't she look yellow to you?"

"Now that you say something, yes she does."

"She has slept most of the day and hardly eaten."

"Really?"

"Yes, I am going to take her down the street to the medical clinic."

"Okay, I am going to rest. Call me if there is anything important."

I put Angela into the car just to go half a block. I bring her into the clinic; they are not equipped to take care of her.

"Mrs. Spaulding, Angela is very sick. We cannot diagnose her here; she needs to go to the Children's Hospital."

"I need to call my husband."

"Sure, use this phone."

I call Paul and he runs to the clinic and we get Angela into the car and to the hospital, which the clinic had called ahead, so we would not have to wait, we were taken the second we walked through the door. They take Angela and we are asked to wait in the waiting room for the doctor to come and talk to us.

"Mr. and Mrs. Spaulding?"

"Yes."

"I have to say that you got Angela help in time."

"What is wrong with her?"

"We did a spinal tap and Angela has beta strep which is hard to diagnose because there are basically no noticeable signs. If it weren't for the jaundice, we would have never done the spinal tap which found the strep."

The doctor proceeds to tell us the possible long and short-term effects. She also tells us how she got it, which was through the birth canal. I had it and passed it onto her, so because I have it, I to needed to see my doctor and be treated for it, but it does not make the mother sick because of the immune system and the mother is just a carrier.

Two weeks is over and we are bringing home a healthy and happy Angela.

Angela is not even a year old yet and we have decided that we want another baby for we want Angela to have a sibling close in age.

It is October 25, 1993 and I am two months and a half months early in labor and I am having twins, due to the positions of the babies, I have to have a c-section. First baby at 7:31pm, 4lbs 12ozs, and 22 inches is Daniel James Spaulding. Second baby at 7:32pm, 5lbs 4ozs and 21 inches is Melody Ann Spaulding.

Melody is a little yellow and I am scared that she is going to have what Angela had, but I am reassured that she is not, that she is just jaundice.

Daniel is having problems breathing. His lungs are not working right when he tries to exhale and needs to be rushed to the navy hospital that is better equipped to take care of him; I only get to see him for a few minutes before they take him.

I have a bad infection and have to stay in the hospital for a week with Melody, Paul goes to the other hospital everyday to be with Daniel.

It has been a week. I get to leave, but I do not get to take any babies home and I am sad. But the first thing I do is go see my Daniel.

Another week has passed and we get to bring home Melody.

It is now another two weeks and finally Daniel gets to come home.

I am so happy, now finally my beautiful twins are home where they belong.

It has been a wonderful month with my three babies at home, oh, my hands are full, but ever so blessed, but I am noticing the twins are not breathing well. I am thinking this is odd that both are having breathing problems.

We take the twins to the children's hospital and even though they were born three months ago, the doctors say they are one month because they were born ten weeks early and are preemies. They take the twins and find they have the RSV Virus, which is a respiratory tract illness.

Therefore, now after another week of hospital stays, the twins are back home and we are packing to move to Narragansett, Rhode Island.

We did not stay very long in Rhode Island, but long enough to fall in love with the place. I am now twenty-six, Angela is three, and the twins are one and we move back to Michigan because Paul is getting out of the Navy and we are headed back home.

On January 16, 1997, three months before my 27th birthday, Bob dies of cancer; I go to the condominium to see Arlene.

Arlene leads me to the bedroom where Bob was laying peacefully on the bed. Arlene left us alone.

I am thinking…wow, I have been to many funerals since my sister died, but I never would visit the body. I would just find a chair in the back and sit until the service was over. This was the first time I actually got close to a dead body. I actually touch Bob's cheek, as I do I say, "I love you dad. Thanks Bob!"

Chapter Nine

"And when the night is cloudy, there is still a light, that shines on me, shine until tomorrow, let it be."
~Let It Be-by The Beatles~

You know there is something very freeing and self-empowering about putting faith in someone/something bigger then you. To say, "This is now out of my hands, it is now up to you do what you will, I will learn," it is a very humbling moment.

It is the end of March 2002; I am going to see David Walton in the nursing home because earlier this month his niece Roxanne told me that David wants to see me to clear the air.

My drive to Battle Creek was a gut knotting experience. I walk into Roxanne's house thinking that I may have to toss my cookies in the bathroom in which Sally died in, for now Roxanne lives at 54 Jericho Road. I go into the living room and suck in the feeling of wanting to throw up because I have decided that I am not going to go into that bathroom.

Roxanne and I get into our cars to go to talk to David. We get to the nursing home and I am thinking about when I used to work in nursing homes as a CENA so I knew anything was possible to see and that nothing would be too gross for me. We walk into his room; I see this lump of clothed sweaty flesh lying there in the hospital bed.

"Hi Nancy, come here and sit on the bed next to me."

"No."

"I won't bite."

"I would rather stand."

"You look scared, there is no need to be, right Roxanne?"

"I have no idea. I am not scared, but I cannot speak for Nancy because she has had a different life with you then I have."

"David, I am fine standing. I got your message that you wanted to clear the air, tell me the truth, and that is the only reason I am here. Now do you want to clear the air or not?"

"Yes, I do, Nancy."

David looks at me, opens his mouth to speak, but all I hear was the same old broken record. Blaming me, saying how horrible Bonnie was, not at all looking at what kind of person he was and is. Not one single breath of truth from those disgusting lips.

"Enough of this crap; I am sick of you and you're accusing lies."

I storm out the room, down the clinical halls, and out the nursing home front doors.

Roxanne catches up with me outside.

"What are you going to do now?"

Looking up at the skies, I throw my hands up into the air.

"God, it is now in your hands. Roxanne, I am just so tired of fighting for answers. I am having surgery in a week and not only that, my kids need their mother; this is no longer up to me. It is up to God."

I get into my car, driving back to Grand Rapids. I now do not have that knotting feeling, I now feel light. A big burden has been lifted off my shoulders. I now know what is, for now if I really want answers, I need to totally 100% trust in something bigger than me.

It is amazing what can happen when you learn to give you problems up to a higher being, whoever that higher being may be, because I now see what can really happen when someone learns that sometimes you need to let go and let your faith in something bigger than you take over.

Two weeks have now passed and I have had a major surgery. Todd Miller and Barb Walters called me today to tell me that they are starting up a Cold Case Team for Calhoun County and that they were going to start with my sisters case. They asked if I could come in for an interview.

"You're going to have to come to my house for the interview, for I cannot drive for a few months due to major surgery."

"Nancy, that is no problem. We have time in two days in the morning to come."

"That is no problem."

It is April 30, 2002, four days after my 32nd birthday. I am getting the kids ready for school, but I am not able to concentrate on the morning routine due to my post-surgery pain.

The kids leave for school, leaving me with my excitement of having the closure that I so need and want. I am standing at my front door, a dark blue car with the State of Michigan emblem on the side door parks on the street, right in front of my middle class home.

As I stand there looking at the state car, I think to myself that as a child when I saw such a car I knew that we were getting a visit from a social worker, and it was time for me to get on the mask that Bonnie had created for me so I could lie to the social worker. Now it pulls up in front of my house, as an adult I wear no mask...all there is now is the truth.

Chapter Ten

"Then one day the sun appears, and we come shining through those lonely years."~I Made It Through The Rain- by Barry Manilow~

You know, when you have been waiting for the truth for almost what seems to be a lifetime, finally here it is, there are so many emotions that hit you all at once. One thing I know for sure, the individuals that bring you that truth become some of the dearest people in your life. These individuals become your friends and a special kind of family to you.

It is May 21, 2002, twenty-one days after my interview; today, Bonnie and David has now been arrested. Sitting in Maria's office, John Hallacy comes in to see how I am doing and to tell me about the arresting moments.

"Hi Nancy, how are you?"

"Okay, numb and a bit in disbelief, but never the less I am okay."

"Well, the arrest went without any problems."

"Good, I am so glad."

"When we went to get David, it took a bit of time, being that he is bed ridden and paperwork needed to be done. I have to tell you, Nancy, it was such a delight to arrest David for when he was rolled out of there lined all the way down both sides of the hall right out the door were doctors, nurses, other staff and residents clapping and cheering. Some of the staff on duty called those who were off and some had enough time to get in to cheer and see David off."

"That is just so awesome, and so heart-warming."

"Bonnie, it only took a few minutes. She was at home, she was handcuffed, and as she walked out to get into the police car, she was sobbing."

"Wow! Thanks everyone from the heart."

Chapter Eleven

"Come on with the rain, I've a smile on my face."
~Singing In The Rain-by Gene Kelly

Mother; noun: 1. female parent 2. maternal tenderness or affection

Parent; noun: **a :** one that begets or brings forth offspring **b :** a person who brings up and cares for another

November 5, 2003; Bonnie's trial is first, which is a bench trail; the judge is Conrad Sindt. The attorneys are asking me some probing questions. It is making me feel as if I am going to space out, but I fight the urge to, so I did not. The prosecutor Jeff Kabot is the first to question me after being sworn in.

"Please state your full name for the court."

"Nancy Marie Spaulding."

"Okay, Ms. Spaulding. I have a few questions for you."

"Okay, I am ready."

"The court will need you to speak louder. Now, Ms. Spaulding, in our transcripts, it says there was a TV show you and Sally would watch."

"Yes."

"Please tell the court what show that was."

"It was 'The I Love Lucy' Show."

"On the night that Sally died, were you watching that at any time during that day?"

"Yes."

"Please tell us about watching the show."

"It was just after Bonnie and David got done beating Sally and putting her in the tub. I sat on the sofa, the show came on, and I watched it. I can even tell you what episode it was."

"Thank you, now I want to ask you, do you remember what Sally was wearing when she was taken to the hospital?"

My heart sunk, for I do have a gift of remembering things in details, but there are times that, when a lot of time goes by, I tend to doubt that gift, but I went with what I always believed and what was in my heart. Therefore, I answer the question.

"Yes I do."

"Please tell us what she was wearing."

"Black and green plaid pants."

Jeff goes to his table for a bit; he pulls out a folder and walks back to me.

"Now, Ms. Spaulding, before I ask the next question, I need to tell you what I am about to show you is very disturbing, but I need to show you this and ask you. "Are these the pants?"

Jeff pulls a picture of Sally lying on the cold silver autopsy table with black and green plaid pants on out of the folder and hands it to me.

"Yes, those are the pants."

I start shaking and crying, because not only seeing Sally dead in the picture, but also her body covered in cuts and bruises and then to top it off my memory was validated. With a victim that has been through as much as I have, validation is ever so important.

"Good job, thank you. Your Honor, I am done with questions of Ms. Spaulding for right now."

Bonnie's lawyer, David Merchant, comes to me to start his questions. He is asking a few that seems to be more like just getting to know each other.

"Okay, Ms. Spaulding, a few more questions."

"Okay."

"How sure are you on the show you were watching?"

"100%."

David Merchant now walks to his table, picks up a piece of paper, and walks back to me.

"Ms. Spaulding, I have here a copy of the TV guide from the date in question. Would you please look at this and tell me what time the I Love Lucy Show came on?"

"Sure."

I am looking over the copy and I cannot find it anywhere, but I am not going to show any expression and hand it back.

"I cannot find it."

"Thank you, Ms. Spaulding. Your Honor, I am done with this witness."

The judge is looking at me and then over at Jeff Kabot.

"Mr. Kabot, do you have anything else?"

"Yes, your Honor, thank you."

Jeff Kabot comes to me with a piece of paper in his hand.

"Ms. Spaulding, you say you are 100% sure of the show you were watching."

"Yes."

"Your honor, I want to bring to your attention that, in 1978, the TV guides did not strictly follow what was really on TV."

He then hands the paper to the judge, goes to his table for another paper and comes over to me.

"Ms. Spaulding, do you remember any interviews after Sally died?"

"Yes, I had a few. One at the police station with Bonnie and David there and then I had an interview with someone at school."

"Okay, I have here a copy of part of the interview you did at school. I want you to read to yourself what is highlighted."

As I read the small part that has been highlighted, I start to cry. I finish reading and hand it back.

"Ms. Spaulding, please tell the court what you told the interviewer back in 1978."

"I told the interview that I was watching 'The I Love Lucy Show'."

I am crying ever so hard for yet another validation. Jeff Kabot is my knight in shining armor for he is giving me some much-needed validation and is proving to me that, if you really know the truth, the truth will set you free. In this case, set my mind free.

"Thanks Ms. Spaulding. Your Honor, I am finished."

The judge looks at David Merchant.

"Mr. Merchant, anymore questions?"

"No your honor, thank you."

I get off the stand and sit next to my victim advocate, Maria Markos. Jeff Kabot gets Maria's attention and they talk for a minute. Maria comes back to me.

"Nancy, I was just told that you cannot sit in the courtroom because you could be called again and if that is possible, then you cannot be in here."

I am so pissed; I get up and grab my water bottle. I am so mad that I go out into the hall, I slam my water bottle on the floor, and it bursts open, spraying water all over like a sprinkler.

I run to the elevator and push the close door button because Maria, who is a person full of passion for her job, is trying to catch up with me along with Heather, an intern that Maria is training.

The doors close. I huddled into the corner of the elevator with my legs pulled to my chest and cry out.

"This is not fair!"

I am thinking that after all these years; I cannot hear Bonnie on the stand. This makes me mad because I deserve to get the answers straight from the horse's mouth.

I am wishing that Cheryl was here at the courthouse with me, but she is sitting in the airport waiting for her flight to Seattle. I go to Maria's office while Maria and Heather are looking around the courthouse for me. I have Cheryl's mobile number so I use Maria's phone to call Cheryl.

After a few minutes on the phone, Heather looks into the office and sees me.

"She's here."

Cheryl is talking calmly to me on the phone while Maria and Heather walk into the office.

"Everything will be okay."

"But Cheryl, it is not right."

"Nancy, you need to remember Jeff is thinking of the case. He cannot let it get jeopardized in any way."

John Hallacy, who is the head prosecutor, came into the office and in so many words kindly repeats what Cheryl just told me, continues to say, "I am sorry. I really do understand and my heart goes out to you."

Wow, this was the second time John Hallacy said sorry to me. The first time was just a few days before Bonnie's trial started.

John came to me and said, "Nancy, after getting all your past records from the courthouse, I looked them over and all I have to say is, I am sorry."

I looked at him confused as I asked, "why?"

"After reading all the reports and hand written notes from caseworkers, you and Sally should have been taken from your family and not given back. I am sorry that the system let you and Sally down."

John apologizing for a system that he was not a part of at the time that I was being abused means a lot. This was the first time someone said sorry to me. This made me feel with my whole heart and soul that it was a true apology.

I go home. I walk through the door so drained. Paul, my husband, has the kids in the living room watching TV, and he watches me sit in a comfortable chair.

"You look drained."

"Very much so, but give me a minute and I will fix dinner."

"Why don't we just go out to eat? Think you have enough energy to do that?"

"Sure, I can handle that, thanks."

Dinner at Red Lobster is done and all I want now is a hot shower and bed.

I wake up thinking as I am dressing, "why am I going even though with this? I cannot be in the courtroom. Oh I know why because, even though I am not in the courtroom, I do get some answers and plus I am not giving Bonnie the satisfaction of finding out I was not there. I am in this until the end.

Cheryl and I walk into Maria's office and she smiles at us.

"I have some good news for you, Nancy."

"What?"

"Bonnie is not taking the stand.'

"Really, she isn't? So, doesn't that mean I can be in the courtroom now?"

"Yes, that is exactly want that means."

As I walk into the courtroom, I see Bonnie talking to her lawyer. Cheryl, Maria, and I sit in the front row of a small courtroom; we end up sitting right behind Bonnie. That is when the smell hits me like a Mac truck.

There is this smell in the courtroom that brings back memories. While I was having these memories, Maria is feeling sick. Being pregnant does not help any for her, so Maria moves to the second row.

I lean over to Cheryl.

"Do you smell that?"

"Yes, what is it?"

"I know that smell anywhere for I went to school many times smelling like that; it is cat urine."

"That is so nasty."

"That is why Maria moved for one knows that cat urine is not good for an unborn child."

See, I have a good sense of humor. Thank God, for that for it is this humor that has helped me get through a lot of bad stuff and now I am using it for these trials. I was also grateful that Cheryl has the same kind of humor; it is so nice to have someone here with me that gets me and my humor. Cheryl looks at me.

"Goodness, if someone bottled that smell, they could make a fortune off Bonnie alone."

"How is that? She lives off the state so the fact is, they would be making their fortune off the state. Now I am talking about the state getting pissed off, but actually, in this case, pissed on."

"Bonnie is trying to make eye contact with you."

"I didn't notice for not only does she smell horrible, she looks just as horrible."

I am forced to smell Bonnie, I am not going to look at her too, for the first sight of her long, dry, salt and pepper hair, and her face, looking like something from the night of the living dead, made me sick to my stomach.

Cheryl looks at Bonnie as if to say, "Why are you trying to get Nancy's attention? After all you did to her, do you really think she wants anything to do with you?"

Cheryl plays the protective mother role when it comes to me. Any look my way from Bonnie, Cheryl just sits in-between Bonnie and me so I cannot see Bonnie looking at me. Cheryl does not want me to feel intimidated by Bonnie's looking at me.

There was a doctor that testified for us, Dr. Joyce DeJoung. I did not get to hear or meet Joyce; I am told that she did an outstanding job.

The first witness I get to hear on the stand is Dr. Thomas Adams, from Michigan State University; he looks so like Santa Claus.

Not only does he play the part with his somewhat snow-white beard and his twinkling eyes, but his smile is so sweet that when he smiles his cheeks round out into high cheekbones. If you just put a little blush onto his cheeks, you would have thought that he had just came back from passing out gifts to all the good little boys and girls.

Dr. Adams goes up to sit on the stand to testify. While he testifies, he gives me a gift. Not a gift for the adult, but the seven-year-old child that is still trapped inside me.

He is talking about all the possibilities that could have happened to Sally. Not only does he tell us because of his studies, he actually put himself into a hypothermia state. He knows from experience.

He goes systematic, minute-by-minute of what happens to the mind and body. As he tells of his experience, I get chills up and down my spine because he is describing to a "T" of what I felt when I was put into an icy cold bath water, right from the chills, numbness right to the point of the feeling of passing out.

This brings comfort to me because, not only does he understand how I felt, he is able to tell it so distinctly. The only difference between the two of us is that Dr. Adams had control to get out whenever he wanted, where as Sally and I had no control. The control was always in the hands of our parents.

Both sides have rested their case, now it is time to go home and wait for the verdict.

As Cheryl drives back to Battle Creek the next day for the verdict, she is preparing me for a not guilty verdict.

"Nancy, now have you thought about how you would feel if the judge would come back with a not guilty?"

"I was up all night with the feeling that Bonnie would get a not guilty verdict."

I am sitting in the courtroom, waiting for the verdict. I am a nervous wreck. Not only that, but I feel as if all eyes are on me. Even though I am so nervous, I feel the warmth of the kind hearts of the Cold Case Team sitting right behind me. Everyone is here to hear what the judge has to say.

Judge Conrad comes in and gives a long reading of his verdict. One moment, it sounds like he is going to say guilty, then the next it sounds like he would say not guilty. These feelings keep going back and forth as if I am being teased.

Finally, the judge says, "I find Bonnie Lee Van Dam not guilty of second degree murder."

The reason is that Bonnie said that she knew that it could cause Sally's death when she held Sally's legs while David held her under the water. If Bonnie said, she knew it "would" and not "could", then Judge Conrad Sindt said he would find Bonnie guilty.

Bonnie cries out in relief as I cry out in disbelief.

Cheryl grabs me, holds me close so that cameras do not get me crying and more importantly so that Bonnie doesn't make eye contact with me.

As she holds me she whispers, "Just because Bonnie was found not guilty doesn't mean that she is innocent."

Bonnie's lawyer gets her out of the courtroom fast as I am led the back way behind the courtroom to Maria's office.

I am waiting in Maria's office. In about, fifteen minutes John Hallacy comes in.

"I am sorry."

"Thank you, it is what it is."

"Nancy, I just want to tell you that when Bonnie was in the elevator crying, she was asked from someone of the courthouse why she was crying. She replied that she got off. The person said in return, 'no you didn't'. Bonnie tells him, 'well, the judge said I was not guilty'. The courthouse person proceeded to tell her that there's a place for people like her and she's going to burn in hell."

"Wow that really was something."

"Well, Bonnie was so upset with this encounter that as she was walking out the door she wasn't paying any attention and ran into the metal frame of the door so hard that she ran down the outside stairs of the courthouse crying."

I believe with my whole heart that the judge did the best that he could; I respect him immensely for upholding the law.

I also believe that if Bonnie had a jury trial, she would have been found guilty.

I get home and I think of Judge Conrad Sindt. I am thinking about how hard this must have been that he is a human, a human with a heart and I know in my heart that this was hard for him. I know that, if I was in his shoes, I would find it hard to struggle with my feelings of knowing that I could find her guilty because most people don't put such emphasis on the power of words anymore versus doing my the job of up-holding our laws and constitutional rights like I am trusted to do.

As an ex-student of history, someone who has always taken a patriotic view on things, someone that in spite of how imperfect our system is, I am proud to be in that system. So I sit down to send Judge Conrad Sindt an email telling him that I am okay and that I understand why his verdict was not guilty and that I have no ill feelings. I also said that I believe that he is an honorable judge for doing his job the right way, by not allowing his feelings to make his decision.

See, I believe that judges have a very hard job, that in order to be fair they cannot allow their feelings to be involved and yet, when a verdict comes down, they are accused of having no feelings. Really, I believe with my whole heart they do, they are just doing their job.

Lying in bed that night, I think back on what was said to Bonnie in the elevator and the words that Cheryl whispered to me after the verdict and I know that now Bonnie must see herself through the eyes of others. How true, for that in itself is worse than any prison, for she has created her own prison and I find closure in that for, someday, Bonnie will have to answer to a higher judge.

It has been a few days since Bonnie's trail. I get on my computer to check my email and I see that in my inbox there is an email from Judge Conrad Sindt. I think, "Wow, I never expected him to reply, but it does my heart good to see that he has." He tells me,

"Thank you for your kind thoughts. I'm very pleased to hear that you are doing well and I hope that will always be the case. Conrad Sindt"

For you see, this judge has a heart, for Conrad did not have to reply. Not only that, he made it personal by signing it Conrad Sindt, not Judge Conrad Sindt. *Judge Conrad Sindt* kept intact his integrity for his job; but *Conrad Sindt* has shown that he is human.

Chapter Twelve

"Breathe, Nancy, remember to breathe. Take a deep breath."
~Michael K. Kivinen-best advice ever from a dear friend~

Father; noun: 1. male figure 2. to care for or look after a child

It's January 7, 2004 and it is the first day of David's trial.

Matthew Glaser, David's lawyer, is doing a good job of upsetting me. He is harshly questioning me, pacing back and forth.

At times, he stops behind David for a few seconds trying to get me to look in David's direction in hopes that I will get intimidated. I do not look at David; I look at Cheryl instead.

"Was David standing or bending over while he was beating Sally?"

"I'm not sure. There were many things going on at once between Bonnie and David. Everything was happening so fast while, at the same time, it seemed to be the longest moment in time."

"You should remember."

He asked the question again, but this time he is putting motions to his question.

"Was David standing (while at the same time making hitting motions with a closed fist while standing) or was he bending over (as he would bend over doing the same hitting motions)?"

He keeps doing this repeatedly while I kept saying every time he asked in this manner, "I am not sure. Look, I'm not going to say anything unless I am sure about my answer."

Jeff Kabot gets a call, a verdict for another case is in, and he needs a recess. Judge Allen Garbrecht gives a twenty minute recess.

I run through the courtroom, out the door crying and hyperventilating. Scenes of the night that Sally was murdered are going through my mind like a slide show, so fast that my mind cannot keep up with the pictures.

I go into the private room that was for me to sit in and Cheryl followed. By the time she gets into the room, I am sitting at the table with my head down sobbing into my folding arms that rest upon the table.

As I sob, Cheryl held me while reassuring me. "Don't you let him do this to you. You go right into that courtroom with your head held high because this is your time. Don't let him take that from you."

This was only the second time in my life that someone really held me while I sobbed. I remember the first being the day the doctor came into the quiet room to tell us that Sally was gone. I then sat in Mrs. Gowen's lap and buried my head into her and sobbed.

We go back into the courtroom to find out that the judge had a talk with David's lawyer while waiting for Jeff to come back. What was said I do not know, but while David's lawyer was finishing questioning me, he stays behind the pulpit, respecting me for the rest of the time.

David does not look at me when I am on the stand. If he is not falling asleep, he is trying to whisper to the second lawyer. I find it a bit funny, but, on the other hand, it is very distracting because I am trying to answer questions and all I hear is David's voice booming through the courtroom. I am tempted to just stop answering the questions to hear what David has to say, but I am unable to because even though we all can hear, it is like trying to understand a toddler.

I say that not because he is not smart, for David is very smart, but because he has a mumbling problem, people tend to judge him as not being smart.

I know David is smart. After all, he is the one that taught me how to use the library's catalog cards to find a book. Not only that, he taught Sally and me how to play chess at the ages of five and four.

The same witnesses that had testified in Bonnie's trial are going to testify in David's too. I get to stay in David's trial after I testify because we know upfront that David isn't going to take the stand.

I am done testifying. The next to take the stand is an officer. He verified that in 2002 he went to 54 Jericho to take pictures of the bathroom and verified the pictures that were showed to him as the ones he had taken.

Now is detective Pete, who interviewed David. Pete goes all over the country doing interviews that he has specialized. He makes you feel as if he is your best friend.

He worked with detective Dennis Mullen of Calhoun County. Dennis was my contact person for years. He was the detective that helped keep Sally's case open so I could have my day in court.

This interview was videotaped, but only Dennis's parts, not Pete's, for this is one of many ways for Pete to gain David's confidence.

Pete is telling us about how he helped David to the bathroom.

"It was quite a sight."

Everyone in the courtroom laughed, but I laughed a little harder.

Pete looks to me like a young Sean Connery. Picture this, Sean Connery helping David, who at the time of the interview looked like a toothpick and who once was overweight and now is obsessed, by holding onto pounds after pounds of chicken skin onto the toilet, then 007 wiping his saggy butt.

I bring my attention back to Pete's words just in time to hear him say, "David says to me, 'this feels so good, other people won't do this for me'."

I laughed imaging David saying that to such a hunk of a man.

Next, we get to watch some of the video, how sad. There is David sitting on camera in a wheelchair, not saying much. But, boy oh boy, bring him a ham and cheese sandwich and he gets so excited as if he were a two year old opening his Christmas present.

David yells out, "oh boy, a ham and cheese sandwich". Then he is brought a cup of coffee, "and coffee too, this is so nice!"

All David could do was think about eating that answering questions fell to the wayside, so he was allowed to eat, and then the interview continued.

David is hard to understand in the video, so the jury members are given a typed out script so they can follow along with the dialogue.

Next on the stand is Dr. Thomas Adams, giving the same testimony as he did in Bonnie's trial.

It is the last day of David's trial and Bonnie testifies for us.

While Bonnie is on the stand, she incriminated herself big time, but she doesn't care.

This reminds me of all the other times she would lie to save her disgusting butt. She would tell the truth when she had nothing to fear, which in this case she doesn't because she can't be tried twice for the same crime…it is the *double indemnity law*.

If only Sally and I would have gotten that kind of reassurance. We feared for our lives, whether we told the truth or not. Here is Bonnie; no matter what she says on the stand, she will come out smelling like roses, and I do not mean that literally.

Court is adjourned for lunch. The jury will take this time to deliberate in hopes that there would be a verdict by the end of the day.

By the end of lunch, we get a call to say that there is a verdict.

Filing back into the courtroom, I notice that once again my Cold Case family is sitting behind me waiting to hear the verdict.

"Do you have a verdict?" asked Judge Allen Garbrecht.

After the foreman stands he answers, "Yes, your Honor."

"And what is your verdict?"

"We find the defendant David Lee Walton guilty of second degree murder."

As a wave of emotions spread through the courtroom, the judge asked, "So say you all?"

"So says us all."

Jeff and Michael go back into the jury room to talk to the jurors. The jurors had told the prosecutors that if Bonnie had a jury trial, and if they were on that trial, they would also have found Bonnie guilty of second-degree murder.

Meanwhile I am in shock, answering media questions in the hall of the courthouse.

"The one thing that this has brought to me is, from the time I was seven up until now, I grieved out of guilt and out of anger. Now I'm grieving out of love, which is what I should have been able to do twenty-six years ago."

It is nine days later and Cheryl and I return to the courthouse to hear David's sentencing and to give my victim impact speech.

As I wait in the hall for the courtroom doors to open, people are talking. My heart begins to race, my palms sweat, and I start hyperventilating. Oh yes, I know these signs. I am having a panic attack. Before anyone notices, I quickly go to my small waiting room set aside for my privacy. I take an Ativan, which my doctor prescribed to help me at moments like this.

Cheryl comes in to let me know that we can go into the courtroom. She notices I am panicking and as she hugs me, "it is almost over, come on, everything will be okay."

We both walk into the courtroom together.

The judge looks at David.

"Mr. Walton, is there anything you want to say regarding sentencing in this matter? This is your opportunity."

"Yes, Judge."

"Go ahead, Mr. Walton."

"I want to say that I loved Sally very much and that when we were together during all of this, Nancy, Sally, Bonnie and I would ride together in my car, and we'd all sing songs. And I wanted to tell you that I am very sorry for what happened, and I wish the night had never happened."

Alright, thank you. Anything else you want to say?"

"No."

"Mr. Glaser, anything you want to say regarding sentencing?"

"Given the conviction, your Honor, the report is adequate."

"Mr. Kabot?"

"Your Honor, back in 1978, Sally Chesebro was six years old. Today, she would be going on thirty-three. At six years old, Sally was already the victim of numerous acts of child abuse by both Bonnie Van Dam and David Walton."

Jeff pauses for a minute and resumes after taking a drink of water.

"You know, children are kind of unique because there are a number of things about children that we as adults don't possess. Certainly, the reliance on parents for love and affection, for protection, and nurturing."

Jeff looks at David and then back at the judge and points with his hand at David.

"Sally got none of those from the defendant. She did not get any of those from her mother, Bonnie Van Dam. Instead, what she got was a life of torture."

"Back on March the 9th, 1978 the torture finally came to an end because on that night this man put Sally Chesebro in a bathtub full of cold water, forcefully held her in that bathtub of cold water, and ended her life."

Jeff takes a few steps back from the bench, looks over at me, and as he steps back to the bench says, "What I have to say really isn't near as important as what Nancy Spaulding has to say today, so I am going to end my comment here."

"The only other thing that I would like to say is that for the time that Sally Chesebro spent in that bathtub, she was struggling against David Walton as he held her down in the tub, dunking her head underneath the water. David Walton's sentence in this case should be as final and as conclusive as the act that he committed on Sally Chesebro that night."

"David Walton has spent twenty-six years out in public, while Sally Chesebro didn't have the opportunity to ever grow up. David Walton should now know and understand what it's like not to have a life and we would ask the court to adopt the recommendation made by the probation department."

Jeff looks over at Maria. Maria nods, signifying to Jeff that I still want to speak.

"My understanding is, Judge, Nancy Spaulding, the sister of Sally Chesebro, would also like to address the court at this time."

I am shaking as I walk to the pulpit. I feel as though my legs are going to drop from under me.

"Good morning, your Honor."

"Good morning."

As I get my things together I say, "Bear with me for a minute, please."

"Sure, Ms. Spaulding."

"Thank you."

"I want to show you something first. Four days before Sally was murdered, she went to Sunday School, to a church where Bonnie and David both were Sunday School teachers. On that day, she wore this dress. I remember it for it is so small and the jacket, this was one of her favorite outfits. I gave this to my grandmother to keep. I have images in my mind of Sally, and pictures, but this is tangible to me. Her hair once fell upon this dress, laid upon her skin, and her DNA once was on this dress. This is my Sally now."

I set Sally's dress on the prosecutor's table next to Mike Jaconette.

"Your Honor, I want you to know that David has been and always will be a selfish person who can't love anyone without strings attached except for him."

I take in a deep breath.

"Not only did Sally deserve to know that David was her father, she also deserved to live a long and happy life. David not only murdered his daughter and my sister, he also murdered a future mother and an aunt." Wiping tears from my cheeks, I continue, "because of David, my children will never get to know their aunt and what a wonderful sweet person she was, and the beautiful woman she could have been."

Mike hands me some tissues. I dry my eyes and wipe my nose.

"Sally and I had dreams to raise our children together, but David came and took those dreams away."

I look over at David.

"I pray for David as I also pray for Bonnie that they find a true, comfortable, and loving relationship with God, and that they come to terms with all they did to Sally and I, so that someday they'll be able to ask for forgiveness of themselves, God and maybe someday, ask for my forgiveness."

I look up at the Judge Allen Garbrecht.

"Your Honor I want to say that, as parents, we should not only teach our children how to be honest, fair, and loving, but we also need to teach our children how to be compassionate, which are things our parents never taught us. They couldn't teach us these qualities because they didn't have these qualities within themselves to love us and if they did love us, then they didn't care one bit to show Sally and I these qualities."

"But Bonnie and David have given me the awesome opportunity to show my kids firsthand the true art of compassion, and for this and only this I thank them."

"Your Honor, David, and Bonnie were blessed with two beautiful little girls and they threw it all away for their own selfishness and sick perversions. Nevertheless, I do believe that God loves David and I love him only because he is a child of God. And, your Honor, I ask that you punish David to the full extent of the law."

"Before I end with my last few words, I would like to read the lyrics from a song that I consider being my life theme song. This is from my heart to the hearts of everyone who cares."

"I Made It Through The Rain" by Barry Manilow

We dreamers have our ways of facing rainy days.
And somehow we survive; we keep the feelings warm.
Protect them from the storm, until our time arrives.
Then one day the sun appears, and we come shinning through those
lonely years.

I made it through the rain; I kept my world protected.
I made it through the rain; I kept my point of view.
I made it through the rain; and found myself respected.
By the others who…got rained on too: And made it through.

When friends are hard to find, and life seems so unkind,
Sometimes you feel afraid, just aim beyond the clouds,
And rise above the crowds, and start your own parade.

'Cause when I chased my fears away, that's when I knew that I could finally say.

I made it through the rain; I kept my world protected.
I made it through the rain; I kept my point of view.
I made it through the rain; and found myself respected.
By the others who…got rained on too: And made it through.

"Your Honor, I also want to say, before the Cold Case started their investigation, for years, I have lived with guilt that both David and Bonnie had put upon me as a child, and that I believed into my adulthood. Every March, I would get in such a low mood and feel guilty."

"One day, I went crying to a dear friend of mine and her words stick with me to this day."

She said, "Nancy, all across the country, many little girls got into nail polish that belonged to their mothers, but only one little girl, on March 9th 1978, was murdered for getting into nail polish."

She proceeded to say, "You were only kids doing what kids do, and kids don't deserve to be murdered for being kids."

I looked over at David and said to him, "May the peace of the Lord be with you David," then looking at the judge, "and thank you, your Honor."

"Thank you Nancy."

"Anything else?"

Everyone says, "No, your Honor."

"All right, Mr. Walton, I've obviously had the opportunity to review the pre-sentence report and sat through all the testimony as well. So I'm certainly familiar with the circumstances surrounding this offense."

The judge looks at David, "To say that the manner in which you treated Sally Chesebro and her sister was repulsive would be a gross understatement. Indeed, in reviewing with this report, I agree with the agent who prepared this report when he said, words simply cannot adequately describe the horrendous nature of the offense."

The judge goes on to tell David, "You caused the death of a wholly innocent six-year old child, and you caused unimaginable anguish in the life of her sister, Nancy. Quite frankly, it's a miracle here today that Nancy Spaulding has made it through the rain."

"Sally didn't deserve to die; her sister didn't deserve to be treated inhumanely by you, her parent."

"Now twenty-five, almost twenty-six, years later, you must suffer the consequences of this incomprehensible conduct."

"After reviewing this report, and considering the evidence presented during the course of the trial, and the circumstances surrounding this offense, I'm sentencing you to serve a term of imprisonment within the custody of the Michigan Department of Corrections for the rest of your life."

I decide to email Judge Allen Garbrecht. I thank him for listening to my story and for upholding the laws. I also tell him that I am okay and not angry.

It is the next day and I check my email to find a reply from Judge Allen Garbrecht. He says to me,

Dear Nancy,

Thanks for the message. I hear many victims share their emotions during sentencing, and it is so heart wrenching. I especially feel for those victims who have not yet been able to get beyond their anger and bitterness, and my hope for them is that one day they will be able to, as you clearly have. Best wishes to you. Judge Garbrecht

Another judge with a heart and integrity!

Afterword

Four months after David's sentencing, Paul left and filed for divorce. The reasons are not important, for some would say it was right and others would say it was wrong. What is important to know is that when you no longer see eye to eye and your paths are so different that there is no right nor wrong; it just is what it is - LIFE.

Neither Paul nor I are bad people, we just needed to go our separate ways in order to grow; for with growth comes learning which brings us to the wisdom of compassion, to love enough in order to forgive.

Now years later, I am happier then I could ever imagine. I have three wonderful children that, in a very short amount of time, will be adults. I know they did not have a perfect mother, but I am a lot better than what my mother was. I hope that my children will be even better then I was. After all, we as parents should want them to be better and smarter than us.

Just think about it, I am a better parent then my mother, and then my children will be better than me, and their children better than them and so on; how wonderful.

I now understand that when it comes to matters of the heart, I am worthy of being loved.

I loved Paul with my whole heart, but looking back, I can honestly say I was not in love with him. I believe that is because we were trying too hard to make the other happy on our level of happiness.

I now understand that it is no one's responsibility to make another happy. It is the responsibility of the individual to be happy.

I now believe that one should go into a relationship with the attitude that you want to share your happiness, not to want someone to make him or her happy. I want a good friendship with the one I love. The friendship is so important to put first because we have no idea what the future holds, but we do know that, no matter what, the friendship is there.

If I had it to do all over again, I would not change a thing, even if it meant having Sally back. I am who I am because of what I went through and I love who I am, a very caring, and loving person.

If you ever find yourself in the dark, do not be afraid, because there is light and you can find it before it is the end. I found the light and it is not the end for me; I have a lot to live for and a lot to love.

I found my light within myself, because I know that I am divinely blessed, and able to bless others, as you are too.

To Rachel and you

A = awesome and you
are great to work
with you!
Remember you are blessed
and able to bless others.

Many Cherbeyla
03/10/2023

Made in the USA
Monee, IL
28 February 2023

28711288R00079